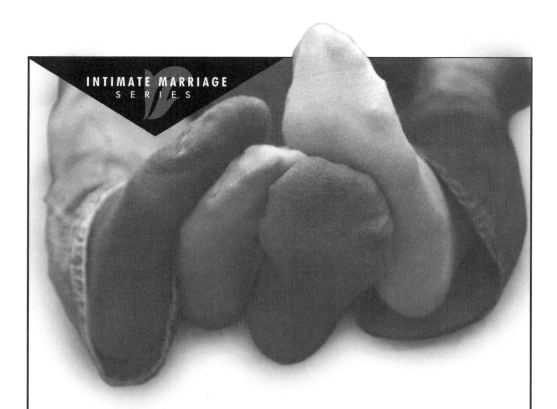

INTIMATE MARRIAGE
SERIES

INTIMATE MARRIAGE
LEADER'S GUIDE

Dan B. Allender & Tremper Longman III

InterVarsity Press
Downers Grove, Illinois

InterVarsity Press
P.O. Box 1400, Downers Grove, IL 60515-1426
World Wide Web: www.ivpress.com
E-mail: mail@ivpress.com

InterVarsity Press® is the book-publishing division of InterVarsity Christian Fellowship/USA®, a student movement active on campus at hundreds of universities, colleges and schools of nursing in the United States of America, and a member movement of the International Fellowship of Evangelical Students. For information about local and regional activities, write Public Relations Dept., InterVarsity Christian Fellowship/USA, 6400 Schroeder Rd., P.O. Box 7895, Madison, WI 53707-7895, or visit the IVCF website at <www.intervarsity.org>.

Unless otherwise indicated, all Scripture quotations are taken from the Holy Bible, *New Living Translation, copyright © 1996, 2004. Used by permission of Tyndale House Publishers, Inc., Wheaton, Illinois 60189. All rights reserved.*

Design: Cindy Kiple

Images: Jean LucMorales/Getty Images

ISBN 0-8308-2129-5

Printed in the United States of America ∞

Library of Congress Cataloging-in-Publication Data

Allender, Dan B.
 Intimate marriage leader's guide / Dan B. Allender and Tremper
Longman III.
     p. cm.
 ISBN 0-8308-2129-5 (pbk.: alk paper)
 1. Church work with married people. 2. Marriage—Biblical
teaching—Study and teaching. 3. Marriage—Religious
aspects—Christianity—Study and teaching. I. Longman, Tremper. II.
Title.
BV4012.27.A45 2005
259'.14—dc22

2005005913

P	23	22	21	20	19	18	17	16	15	14	13	12	11	10	9	8	7	6	5	4	3	2	1
Y	23	22	21	20	19	18	17	16	15	14	13	12	11	10	09	08	07	06	05				

CONTENTS

HOW TO USE THIS BOOK

Welcome! This leader's guide is designed to be your companion through the Intimate Marriage Bible Study series.

In the first three chapters you will find information on why we wrote this series and how to lead a couples small group.

In chapter four you will find additional background and helps for leading the sessions in each of the seven Bible study guides.

And in chapter six you'll find a series of four sermons that cover the key themes of the Bible study guides. These can be used to bring together the whole church around this topic.

So feel free to move around the book, using the parts that are helpful to your situation.

On the InterVarsity Press webpage for the Intimate Marriage Series, you will also find printable flyers and posters you can use to promote this series in your church as you start up small groups or a churchwide marriage emphasis. Visit <www.ivpress.com /title?2130> and click on the IVP Extra link.

If you are wondering whose voice is the "I" at various points, it may help you to know that Dan Allender is the primary writer of chapters one through four, and Tremper Longman is the primary writer of chapters five and six. We hope that our lives and experience will be an encouragement and help to you in your journey.

1

A MARRIAGE MOVEMENT

I sat with a dear friend, a strong believer, whose marriage had just come to an end. He wept. I did too. I felt sick, furious and helpless. He will soon be a marriage statistic, a member of the over 50 percent of failed marriages.

His wife had cavalierly sauntered away from the marriage. As he told me the story of the relationship, I sat silent in outrage at her disregard. Though I eventually put words to my anger and heartache, there was really nothing I could do to "save" his marriage, protect him from harm or make sense of the end of a nearly thirty-year marriage.

He is a victim of our culture's ongoing march away from fidelity, integrity and commitment. However, he is not an *innocent* victim. He brought much harm to the marriage through his flight from conflict. He refused to fight for his disintegrating marriage, thinking he was loving his wife by ignoring many signs that indicated relational disease. He had persistently refused to plunge into the unknown, to name failures of love and confront problems in their relationship. Eventually his lack of courage and her disinterest ate away the body of the marriage like cancer.

When a marriage ends, there are no innocent victims. Even when a marriage is destroyed through an obvious violation like an affair, there is always more to the story. Divorce is a tragedy with no winners.

I firmly believe that it takes two to make a good marriage, but it is possible for one person to ruin it. This sad fact doesn't deny that in all marriages there are two sinners. Yet one person can, by their perfidy or hardness, destroy a way for a marriage to be restored. And further it is imperative that one understand that simply because both partners are sinners, it is not the same to say that a spouse who was unfaithful or abusive was caused to do so by the other's sin. This is heresy to say or to assume.

The spouse who was wronged may have been a healthy, growing person, courageous to pray, forgive, explore problems, risk attempts at intimacy and seek outside help. Where the offending spouse was not willing to do the work and open up to transformation, the person who did hard work is a victim and often a hero in his or her efforts to love and restore the marriage.

No doubt you will eventually be caught in the complex web of marital dissolution. Our efforts to nuance the stickiness will help little in the swirl. Your calling is to remain faithful to seek truth as it can be found and remain involved and hopeful for those who suffer great loss through the process of divorce.

Further, the children of a divorcing couple are innocent victims. To claim a divorce benefits the children or each other is self-deception. It is simply not true. A divorce may be necessary, but it always brings a new level of damage that is almost impossible to take into account.

Who is at fault in my friend's divorce? The answer certainly begins with the wife who left. But my friend, her husband, must also be held accountable. He failed to pursue help for the disease ravaging his marriage. But truth be told, I too am implicated. In an important sense I bear responsibility. After all, they were friends of mine. I recognized failures of love but said very little. I didn't say what needed to be said until long after the dissolution of the relationship had begun. When a divorce occurs, it is natural, but unhealthy, to blame others. First and foremost we are called to examine the log in our own eye.

- Did we fail to speak when we saw failures and troubles in our relationship, or our friend's relationship?

- What is the quality of our marriage? Do we invite others to honesty, humility and hope by the way we live in our marriage?

- What are we doing to build, support and strengthen marriages in our neighborhood, community and church?

It is too easy to justify ourselves: "Well, I was afraid to offend our friends by offering an observation about another person's marriage. I didn't want to appear to be a busybody." Or perhaps we excuse ourselves by thinking, *I barely have time to sit with my own spouse, let alone be concerned about how other couples are doing. Honestly, what can one person do to stem the tide of such a malignant culture?*

The following advice may seem to aim low, but heeding it has potentially tremendous effects: Talk with two couples about what you have learned from God about marriage, and then invite them to do the same—to support two other couples. Imagine the results if everyone who reads this guide takes action in this small way. In an amazingly brief time, legions of marriages will be touched by truth and hope!

But what is it that we are to teach ourselves and others? And once we figure out what it is, how do we communicate with others?

The package you've opened up provides some tools to wage war against the cancer that is destroying marriages.

1. *A book on marriage.* *The Intimate Mystery* focuses on the biblical account of God's establishment of the institution of marriage in Genesis 2:18-25. In particular, it explores the core concepts of the divine command for a couple to *leave* previous loyalties, to *weave* a new life together and to *cleave* together in sexual union. The book is not a how-to manual but rather brings readers on a hike to an outlook spot with a spectacular view, where they can get the big picture of the terrain they must traverse to reach the destination of the marriage feast of the Lamb.

We strongly recommend that each couple in a Bible study own one copy of the book and use pens or markers to underline passages that intrigue or call for further reflection and discussion. It is ideal if the book is read before the Bible study sessions begin or early in the process.

2. *A series of Bible studies.* There are seven booklets with six Bible studies in each one. The studies examine the nitty-gritty joys and pains of marriage through the prism of significant Bible passages and are designed for use in a Bible study group. It is best if each member of the study group owns their own booklet. Obviously, it is preferable for the individuals and couples to go through the passages well before the start of the group Bible study.

However, a study group is only one possibility for the use of the material. A single couple can use the booklets to work through the topics together. Even couples that do well in communication and enjoy their sexual life could enrich their marriage by studying those topics together. Or one partner may do well to study an issue alone first before attempting to address the concerns with her or his spouse. In short, a study group, a couple or an individual may use the material profitably.

> *Imagine the results if everyone who reads this guide takes action in this small way. In an amazingly brief time, legions of marriages will be touched by truth and hope!*

We can't prescribe how best to teach the material in the Bible studies. It is perhaps ideal for it to be done by a couple, both for modeling a fallible-but-honest marriage and to facilitate one-on-one addressing of knotty problems that surface in the course of group meetings. A female leader shouldn't be the one to follow-up with a man who admits to a pornography problem; a male leader shouldn't call a female member to talk about struggles with addiction or confession of having had an abortion. There may be some situations where a single person or one partner in the marriage may teach the material, but with some loss if done alone. We would rather have the material taught than to presume that it should not be done unless it is taught by a couple.

We also believe this material will have enormous impact for good if taught in a women's-only or a men's-only Bible study or accountability group. Obviously, it will be taught only by one partner in this setting and will miss some of the depth and richness of a both-spouses group, but it can gain the value of an intimate discussion that sometimes happens when one's spouse is not present to react.

Thankfully, we don't know what is best; therefore, it is the privilege and responsibility of those teaching to configure the context for the maximum effect for good.

To delve deeply into the Bible's wisdom on marriage, a group could make a year-long study out of these seven booklets. If that is not possible, we strongly suggest that the study begin with the first guide, *The Goal of Marriage*, and proceed to at least one other to allow couples to get into some of the hard work of growing their marriages in community.

3. *A leader's guide.* This leader's guide provides a road map and an itinerary to help you take your group from ground level to the destination of strong, humble and hopeful

marriages. No map can serve the same end as an experienced guide, but using the guide can extend your confidence to serve as a group leader by helping you avoid some obvious pitfalls and to know that group struggles, like conflict in a marriage, are neither surprising nor a failure but are to be expected—and they are necessary if growth is to occur. This guide will identify some key principles for helping people grow, what is required to be a good leader, how to run a fruitful group with agreed-upon goals, and how to deal with the unexpected with grace and wisdom. In addition, we provide a series of sermon outlines for those who wish to use this study series as a more formal church initiative with pulpit support.

4. A DVD. Taking into account the fact that ours is a visual culture, the accompanying DVD introduces the core concepts of the book and Bible study series through presentations by Dan B. Allender. It is our hope that uniting word and image will make possible a stronger learning experience. The DVD is an excellent summary and guide to what we hope readers and participants will gain from the whole series and each study guide. The DVD also contains interviews with married couples that highlight marital issues addressed in the study guides.

Divorce is ravaging lives. It calcifies the hearts of legions of children and shreds the fabric of our culture. Personally, I don't know if I can bear another friend's divorce. Staying involved in marriages that are fraying and maintaining hope for couples in the middle of their darkness means enlisting in spiritual warfare.

This leader's guide, the marriage book, the seven Bible study guides and the DVD represent Tremper's and my efforts not only to curse the darkness but also to light a candle of hope for marriages, no matter how hard the winds of evil blow. For this reason, it is imperative to understand what is different about this series.

SIMPLE AND DEEP

We don't need more self-help principles to make marriages work.

For the last several decades the Christian community has wallowed in the self-help morass of so-called practical, doable principles. Culturally we are a demanding people, short on time and energy to reflect. We want answers. We want answers to complex problems—now. This drives us to seminars that offer a series of "answers" and techniques for better communication, conflict resolution and sex. When long-term change doesn't happen even though we followed the steps, we are left even more hopeless than when we began to seek for help. If the experts can't help, what is my solution? What is my hope? For many, the only hope is to flee marital problems by getting more involved with their job, children or church. To flee may add some time to a dying marriage, but it only increases the desperate feeling that no change is possible.

It is not enough to complain about the social ills of our time. It is certainly not wise to wax nostalgic about the supposed innocence and goodwill of former times. We can no more put the genie back into the bottle or close Pandora's box than we can make our bodies younger by better diet or exercise. We must embrace our time and place and ask, *What am I to do now?*

Perhaps a generation ago church leaders could assume that marriages would last, with only a few exceptions. Today it is far more realistic to assume that every marriage in the church will end or lose its luster due to disregard. Certainly they all will end in disaster unless they are redeemed—intentionally and often. Redemption does not come by merely offering couples a few helpful hints or a handful of biblical-sounding principles. More must be done, far more, than to teach better how-to techniques.

Redemption does not come by merely offering couples a few helpful hints or a handful of biblical-sounding principles.

We must get down to the foundation on which God calls us to build our marriage. That foundation is encapsulated beautifully in Genesis 2:24. This brief statement joins together three core principles: *Leave* your mother and father. *Weave* a union of emotional and spiritual intimacy. *Cleave* in sexual union—pure, pleasurable and without shame. To understand and accomplish this is both amazingly simple and deep.

In our self-help, tell-me-what-to-do-now culture, we are allergic to concepts that don't immediately make sense or don't provide clear instructions for what to do. For example, what does it mean to leave one's mother and father? Such leaving is not geographic. It is not merely financial. It involves a far more subtle question: To whom do I give my greatest loyalty? Is it to my past and my parents or to my spouse? Your Bible study group will include couples who have been married for decades but have never pondered that question or considered whether they have truly left their parents. Some will want to dismiss the question as either too obvious and simplistic or too foreboding and deep. It is our task in this study to help people see both the glorious simplicity of God's commands and the enormous depth of his plan, which will take a lifetime and beyond for any of us to comprehend.

HONEST AND HOPEFUL

We must tell the truth in a context where the story of our marriage is being encouraged toward a glorious destination.

There is one central truth this series is founded on: *already and not yet.* That is, we live in the period between the resurrection and the second coming. Evil remains, yet its destruction is sure. Christians are becoming holy, but we still sin against God and others. Our glorification is assured, but it is not yet a reality.

Many theologians have underscored this truth, sometimes to remind us that we are both saints and sinners. We are redeemed, yet we await redemption. This provides real relief for my marriage, opening a space where I can simultaneously be honest and hopeful. My marriage is a mess because my spouse and I are both sinners. But it will one day be glorious because we are both saints.

Honesty and hope must go together. If I am hopeful without being honest, I am a blind optimist. Without honesty, I simply won't tell the truth about myself, my spouse or our marriage.

On the other hand, if I am honest about problems but have no hope, then my eyes will be wide shut. I see the struggle and the problems, but I have no imagination to risk what seems impossible. The consequence of truth without hope is a rejection of redemption.

If I am already saved, then I can embrace hope in spite of my and my spouse's sin. Knowledge of my redemption will allow me to name the truth about my sin, no matter how horrific or dark it seems. If I hold together honesty about my sin and certainty of my future redemption and live by this dual light, then I have a foundation on which to build a strong marriage.

If my wife and I live in isolation from community, there is not enough fiber to our relational rope to resist the inevitable and incessant strain and fraying. We need other married couples to help save and grow our marriage.

But it is not easy to engender and keep in mind the twin realities of an already-and-not-yet redeemed life. Fortunately, the Christian life is not to be lived alone. We face the truth about our failures and hope for a more glorious future in community. That is why this series is best taught and learned in the midst of fellow sufferers and sojourners.

In our day it's not enough to read a book on marriage or attend a conference as a couple. If my wife and I live in isolation from community, there is not enough fiber to our relational rope to resist the inevitable and incessant strain and fraying. We need other married couples to help save and grow our marriage. It's for this reason that we wrote this curriculum to be lived out in a small group. You see, this is not to be conceived as an ordinary small-group Bible study that focuses on marriage. Instead it is intended to be a catalyst for profound personal transformation. Its purpose is to help couples wrestle with the insidious external and personal factors that could rob them of their memories and future.

Four core assumptions about marriage have guided our labor.

- Marriage is the primary context to raise children, reveal God and restore the culture.
- No marriage is perfect. Some are in deep trouble, teetering on the edge of divorce; others seem peaceful. But even stable marriages struggle and need transformation.
- Marriages are seldom transformed by spouses' trying a few new ways to spice up romance, communicate better or spend more time together.
- Marriage transformation requires deep and frequent encounters with the gospel, which exposes the heart and draws us back to the one fountain that can quench our thirst.

The utmost desire of our heart is to provide resources for you to create a marriage movement. In our day the mere dissemination of information is not enough. We need more than information; we need a life-transforming encounter with the person of Jesus, the Word of God. Thus a marriage movement in your church must go well beyond the conventional yearly focus on marriage that many churches carry out.

How can such a movement begin?

The Spirit of God must work in our midst. True transformation can never occur without the conviction and healing that come from the blessing of the Spirit, not the fruit of mere human labor. Still, there are things we can do to lay a strong foundation for deep personal change.

First, we must tell the truth. We must tell the truth about marriages, including our own. Many will hesitate: "I can't keep my job or the respect of the leaders in the church *and* tell the real truth." For some, this is a cop-out. They can tell the truth, but they don't want to. For others, it is a tragic reality. If they told the truth of their marital struggles, it would be held against them.

Unquestionably we live in an era of spin. We don't admit to faults, we simply have flaws. We don't own our flaws. We refuse to think they are the result of our own doing. Rather, they are the result of our personality type or the consequence of poor parenting. It is amazing how little we name sin. This series starts with the premise that all marriages are deeply flawed, even good ones. And every core flaw comes from our refusal to face and wrestle with the log in our own eye. If we are to grow beyond the complacent and the comfortable, we'll have to get dirty with the truth. We'll have to take off the silly façades we hide behind to keep others—or ourselves—from seeing how deeply we need grace today.

Thus we need to warn you clearly and soberly: *If you don't want to tell the truth about yourself, others and God, then close this book and look for another marriage series.*

In an adaptation of the well-known U.S. Marines slogan, the marriage movement is "looking for a few good marriages." And the only truly good marriage is one that recognizes that it is not good. It is a terrible oxymoron to be called a "good Christian," for good Christians know they are bad Christians. In the same way, a "good marriage" is one that acknowledges how terribly far it has to grow. Marriage is made up of two sinners who, no matter how mature, are always a long, long way from God and yet so very near when both can say, "I believe, help my unbelief."

> **All marriages are deeply flawed, even good ones.**

What is most odd and most glorious about biblical honesty is how deeply it fills the heart with hope. If hope is based on performing a series of steps or doable principles, it inevitably leads to pride and arrogance: "We know the rules, and we have the strength (of course with God's help) to pull it off." This may sound biblical, but it is the diabolical counterfeit; it is legalism and self-righteousness.

The humility of failure combined with the desire for redemption fuels a desperate hope for God's presence and a wonder and gratitude when our lives match his desire. This is true hope and not the self-righteous counterfeit. The more honest I am about my mess as I align myself with God's grace, the greater will be my gratitude. And the more grateful I am for my spouse, no matter how he or she exposes my need for the cross, the better our marriage will become. Honesty and true hope are soul mates.

What will this mean for you? The answer, like the gospel, is far more than you bargained for. If you are a control freak who needs to know each turn in the story ahead of time, then you ought to either run for your life or anticipate your life being transformed. We ought not plunge into the heartache, disappointment and struggle that dwell in every human heart, and therefore every marriage, without an awareness that we are walking where angels fear to tread.

Does this sound too dramatic? It is no more dramatic than the gospel itself. God intends to change us and often does so in a surprising way. We can't anticipate how he will work in our life. To embark on this study is to enter the complex labyrinth of the soul. Every time I lead a group in discussing the matters of the heart in marriage, I begin with the same prayer: "Lord, merciful and kind, be with us."

Why would any reasonably bright person choose to churn up these difficult waters? Why not try to avoid the struggle? The answer is quite simple: We love redemption. We love drama. And we were made for the biggest battle of the ages, the battle against evil as it works to destroy the core fighting unit—a husband and wife. If you choose this Mission Impossible, you are in for the run of your life and the glory of the life to come. Who would be fool enough *not* to jump in?

SINGULAR AND COMMUNAL

A redemptive approach to marriage must begin where people are rather than expect them to already be where they will one day end up.

What if a husband won't attend a Bible study? He may say he is too busy or he just can't add another commitment to his crowded schedule. This may be a true and wise response. It may be, however, that he is using busyness as an excuse to avoid seeing that his marriage is fragile. He may be struggling with sins that he does not want exposed. He has secret passions that are a deeper pleasure and commitment than his marriage, and to participate in a group might mean his life will start coming apart at the seams.

It takes only one spouse to change a marriage.

Obviously no one can read another's heart fully and accurately, but a leader is wise to remember that not everyone attending a Bible study who promises to tell the truth and seek to grow his or her marriage is really committed to doing so. We are a mix of people with very mixed motives. And we must begin with each person and marriage where it is.

The Marriage Movement holds that it takes only one spouse to change a marriage. While it certainly takes two who share a common goal and God to make a marriage glorious and redemptive, it takes only one to start the ball of redemption rolling. For that reason, we believe that a spouse acting on his or her own can benefit from this study. If that person grapples with what God calls them to be and do, a momentum will begin that will unnerve and disrupt the comfort of the other. Once the disruption occurs, more meaningful dialogue and engagement can ensue. The transformation of one will always lead to change for the two.

Sadly, there are times when the other refuses to bless such a transformation and uses it to justify growing more distant from the pursuing spouse. If the faithful spouse continues to love the partner, more conflict will ensue, bringing either repentance or deeper hardness and distance. It is possible that the hardening may lead to a dissolution of the marriage.

It is our conviction that our commitment must not be to our marriage but to our spouse. There are many who keep their marriage intact by surrendering honesty and integrity. For example, if your spouse is physically abusive, it is imperative to have him or her arrested. There is no place for violence in one's home. If your spouse threatens you or physically harms you, then the police need to be called and a process established to provide the offending spouse with help and hope. What you must *not* do is stay in the marriage on the basis of an apology and empty promises to change.

The cost of calling a spouse to grow may be her or his refusal to remain in the marriage. As tragic as that is, it is even worse to remain in a marriage that is founded on lies, denies the hope of the gospel, and sinks into despair and denial.

Thus the transformation of one will inevitably alter the contours of a marriage. But it is always best to study the Bible and life in community. The community may consist of only a dear friend who works through the study with you because your spouse refuses to do so. It is better, of course, if the community is made up of several close friends who join with their spouses to study the Bible together. We hope there will be more than just a handful of couples who do these studies together.

It would be ideal if there were young and old couples. It would be glorious if a group included couples of different ethnicities and life experiences. We would love for groups to make room for couples who are happy and some who are miserable. And why not include folks who are in the process of divorce or recently divorced but open to reflecting on what brought about the dissolution?

The truly adventurous could use these guides in an evangelistic neighborhood Bible study. The studies are designed to help you accomplish whatever you set your imagination to achieve for God. Why not use these studies for engaged couples or those only recently married? Or they could be used on a college campus with men and women who know they'd like to be married and want to prepare their hearts for the challenge that lies ahead. Nothing could be better than to engage these issues before they become a reality.

This study series is humbly designed to transform hearts and marriages. It is written to offer a plan that is as grand and glorious as the gospel. Use it for glory, and be prepared for transformation.

2

COUNTING THE COST
OF LEADERSHIP

Few things in life are more humbling than running for public office, raising adolescents or leading a small group. All three enterprises are guaranteed to expose your weaknesses and challenge your strongest gifts. Leadership is not for the faint-hearted, and leading a marriage-oriented small group is an ideal challenge—for those who find themselves bored with bungee jumping!

Leading a marriage group is more frightening than bungee jumping? No doubt many readers will consider this an excessive claim. Actually, it's possible to lead a danger-free marriage study. It all depends on how you run the group and what you want to accomplish. For example, it's possible to lead any Bible study with a simple fill-in-the-blank approach. This is the standard fare in many groups over the years because it requires little of the leader or the group members. Or, you might focus on the kinds of goals held by some Sunday school teachers of four-year-olds: First, keep fights from breaking out, and second, keep the group on task. When a diversion occurs, redirect your adult group by pointing to the need to finish within the allotted time to keep momentum going.

In a risk-free group, there is little personal application, group discussion or accountability. However, knowledge is disseminated, and satisfaction is guaranteed—if the goal is simply completion of the study. The studies we've created can be approached in this fashion, but to do so would be to wrench them from their relational context and force them into a mere information-gathering box. We don't think this is a strong learning environment (for children or adults).

The Intimate Marriage series is meant to be transformational; therefore it requires a leadership approach that is different from that used in many Bible study groups. Leadership here will call you to be honest about your struggles while honoring the limits that other couples may wish to retain as they participate in the group. It will also require you, the leader, to set strong boundaries of protection for marriages in which one partner wishes to share more than the other does. You may have to grapple with an even more challenging situation: when one spouse dumps frustrations and hurts relating to the other in the group, a public context where they may feel like being more honest than they are in private.

It is safe to say: many marriages are a mess. And even good marriages have tough issues that easily can undermine their core strength and expose significant disappointment and desire. The moment one begins to talk about marriage, there is a big risk of a storm surge. Leadership in this context requires more than in other groups. This chapter will focus on what is required of the leader to lead this group well.

WALKING THE TALK

It may seem absurdly obvious, but if you lead a group through part or all of these guides, it is imperative that you love your spouse and have a good marriage. But be careful. What we mean by a good marriage and what is typically classified as a good marriage may be two different things. So what do we mean by a good marriage? What are its core qualities? A good marriage

- experiences great joy and sorrow through the ebb and flow of life
- brings a taste of both heaven and hell to both spouses
- plans and pursues personal and corporate growth
- increases a desire for heaven and a hunger to repent
- refuses to remain stuck in any rut or ritualized patterns
- seeks the best for each other
- rises above petty, self-absorbed demands
- rejects contempt, demeaning language and behaviors, and violence of any kind
- names failure without loss of hope or bitterness
- notices when intimacy is stale and romance has cooled
- risks to move into deeper levels of communication and care
- moves each partner into deeper service for the gospel

After reading this list, you may well ask: "Are there *any* good marriages?" But remember: a good marriage is honest, intentional and open, and it doesn't take another decade to be honest—one simply needs to admit that it is easier to distort the truth and run. The paradoxical truth is that the moment we admit that we are not very honest,

The paradoxical truth

is that the moment

we admit that we are

not very honest,

we've become much

more truthful.

☛

we've become much more truthful. In the same way, as we give up the easier path of just letting things happen and instead make a plan to engage, we have become intentional. To ask God to sweep away our defensiveness brings a new level of openness to the process. Again, this does not take a decade: a good marriage can become a great one in a very short time.

To walk the talk is to say to each other, "We have no right to lead this group, but we will by the grace of God. And by the sweat of our brow and at the risk of greater loneliness, we will plunge into growing our marriage as we invite others to grow their relationship."

OPENNESS TO MUTUAL EXPOSURE

The cost of walking the talk is to open yourself to being exposed. You can't lead these studies by simply doing the homework prior to the group meeting. A quick perusal of the answers prior to the meeting is not enough. One of the great requirements of running this group is allowing your marriage to be a model for what not to do, and for what to do when your marriage is troubled by the truth.

If your marriage is a model of how to live, then it is best to run this group with sinless participants. Actually, if what you offer the group can be condensed in the slogan

Live like Us

and You Can Be Happy, Prosperous and Content

then you should not lead these studies. If you are not still wrestling to know God and to live out truth, then it is likely that you are offering not the gospel but a version of self-righteousness. There are many other approaches to marriage that will enable you to offer that hubris as a form of spirituality, but this series will not.

We ask that you be a model of redemption. A model of redemption is as free to name sin and death as to name resurrection. To lead these studies you don't need to be in a perfect marriage—just a marriage that can tell the truth.

The truth is we are still sinners. Each of us still struggles with lust and anger. Or to apply what Jesus says in Matthew 5:21-28 to my marriage, both my wife and I struggle with adultery and murder. What is wrong with our marriage? My wife is married to an *adulterer* and a *murderer*. And so am I.

It is possible to dismiss what I've just said as not true for you or your marriage. Many might say with great indignation, "I've never committed adultery and certainly never taken another person's life." I am grateful you don't need to take my word for it: this is the word of Jesus. He is the one who takes such a radical view of sin.

If you have ever desperately desired something other than God to fill up your empty heart, then you know lust. If you have ever wanted to make someone pay for having hurt you, then you know anger. And Jesus names the experience of lust as adultery and unrighteous anger as murder. Every marriage is marked by the tragedy of adultery and murder. If we fail to name it, we fail to see our need for grace today. If we fail to see ourselves and our spouse as struggling with adultery and murder, then we will not recognize what God wants to transform in ourselves, let alone in our marriage.

I, Dan, have been married to Becky for twenty-eight years, and our marriage has grown through thick and thin, yet we are nowhere near the finish line of maturity. We will be struggling as a couple and as individuals up to the moment we pass into another world. We will be growing until the day we die. Thus there is always more we can confess and say about growth.

To lead a group through this series, a couple needs to be willing to share *something* about where they are and where they would like to be. It doesn't require complete, full honesty (even if such a thing were possible). Let me reiterate this last point. To lead this group a couple doesn't need to reveal all their private and personal struggles. We recommend only that you be willing to let the group see some of the realities of the life of a couple committed to transformation.

> **If we fail to see ourselves and our spouse as struggling with adultery and murder, then we will not recognize what God wants to transform in ourselves, let alone in our marriage.**

TIME TO TALK

Transformation doesn't happen on cue. It doesn't happen because you have worked through the lesson several days before the group meets. It is best to consider Luke 14 before you embark on leading a marriage study group. In that chapter Jesus says that a person intending to build a tower or go to war must first "count the cost." He could easily have added, "Count the cost before you lead a group on marriage."

Please believe us. In no way are we trying to talk you out of leading this group. It is simply wise to know that in leading through your marriage, you will need to be intentional about talking with your spouse.

It would be awful to get into the group and divulge something about your marriage that you've not talked about with your husband or wife. It would be even worse to be asked a question and answer untruthfully, so that your spouse is caught between supporting your lie, or not-quite-truth, and exposing you in the group with his or her profound disagreement.

That is why before each group meeting, you'll need to spend time talking together about your marriage prior to the group and identify the stories that can be told, the matters that are not open for discussion, and *why* one story or fact can be told but another is not open for disclosure.

Here is a cardinal rule: *If your spouse wants something to be kept private, then it must be held in confidence no matter how profitable it would be for the group to know about.*

The only way to honor this rule is to talk beforehand about what is available for discussion and what is not. Often this discussion will prompt more discussion, debate and conflict. That can be good. During these discussions both spouses need to honor all the principles of the *Communication* study guide in this series.

Be sure to carve out at least an hour to two hours, several days before the study, to spend in conversation with your spouse. You may find that one of the greatest benefits of leading these studies is the impetus to it provides to spend time talking together.

STRENGTH TO SAY NO

Later in this leader's guide we will discuss how to handle complex issues that arise in the group. One of those issues will be when a person or couple begins to disclose matters that are too personal for the context or expresses conflict that can't be resolved within the group's time frame. There are ways to handle these moments that help the couple, increase confidence in your leadership and build intimacy in the group. But it all depends on courage, not on technique or mere words.

You must be able to step into the middle of a complex moment and say no. You must have the ability to say, "No, we will not go down a path that is too dangerous or too demanding for the hike we are on." There is no shame in setting boundaries, yet many people fail to do so even with their own children or spouse and thus find it near impossible with others.

To lead this group, you will need to establish clear guidelines, goals and group norms.

A later chapter will cover how to do this. To do so requires you to do more than merely "facilitate" the meeting. Many group Bible studies have taken the dumb-and-dumber approach to leadership, requiring the leader to be just a facilitator who says, "Hey, guys, let's gather around and pray." Then he or she lets the group find its own way through fill-in-the-blank questions.

That may work when the issues are not so personal. Matters relating to one's own marriage are far more volatile and charged with hurt, fear and confusion. Most couples will not indulge in inappropriate disclosure or conflict, but a leader ought not be surprised when there is a meltdown. At such points you must be able to stop the process, name the boundaries that have been agreed to by all the couples, and then formulate a plan for where to go for both the couple and the group. It requires skill, but even more, it requires courage.

> *It all depends*
>
> *on courage,*
>
> *not on technique or*
>
> *mere words.*

PASSION TO PRAY

It may seem obvious, but the greatest gift you give to the group is to pray for it. You will find that you pray often for yourself and the process of the group meeting. But to do so well, you will need to bring each person and couple before the face of God.

Even in a group where self-disclosure is limited, you will be amazed how much you learn about couples simply by being with them. We leak the truth. The way a person jokes about sex or subtly undermines his spouse is not difficult to see. We may choose to ignore it, or we may not know what to say, but we can always bring these matters before God in prayer. A funny thing about prayer: the more we name a matter of concern before God, the more he invites us to step into those turbulent waters. That may be why we tend not to pray.

We need to pray before the members of the group arrive for the meeting. We need to pray before we step into the discussion. We may need to stop during the study to pray. We need to pray as we conclude. And then prayer has just begun.

The most important prayer happens as we hold our concerns about each person and couple before God as we shower in the morning or make our commute to work. If we allow the lives of those in the group to take root in our heart, we will find that prayer is a form of consciousness that ponders the other before God as we ask him to intervene and transform the heart.

It is crucial to establish in the group a mindset of prayer. It is not enough to end each meeting by inviting prayer requests. Even in a marriage group it is rare for someone to ask for prayer for their marriage, or for themselves in their marriage. The ante has to be raised by the leader's asking for the kinds of prayer that he or she hopes will be embodied in the group. Remember this truth: *The group will never go beyond the sacrifice of the leader.*

If you will not ask for prayer regarding significant struggles in your marriage, no one else will. Even if you do, weeks may pass before any one else is willing, and in some groups it will still not happen. This is part of the loneliness of a leader. I have poured my heart out and had no response. I've asked for prayer regarding deep wounds and wars in my soul and had people politely pray an officious, distant recitation.

Of course you will second-guess yourself. You will doubt your wisdom and propriety, perhaps even your sanity. But you are blazing a path, a pioneer in matters of honesty, humility and hope. Someone must go first. And it is you.

I find more often than not, though, that if I humble myself, others will follow. In fact, often I am humbled as others begin to go further and deeper than I expected or desired. By leading, we are inviting others to lead us as well.

If prayer becomes tedious and perfunctory as a group process, it is wise to ask: "How are you all feeling about our time of prayer? Is it meaningful? Do you come anticipating the opportunity to pray, or is it just an expected formality? If it is and you are not pleased with it, what would you like to do with that part of our time?"

Prayer, like sex,

is the most intimate

of connections with

another.

In one group a person responded, "I don't really trust anyone to really know what I need, and I don't know if that is my problem or a reflection of the group, because I don't tend to let people know what I need if it really matters to me." Her honesty changed our time of prayer. All it took was for someone to admit how hard it was; subsequently prayer became a far richer part of our time together.

Prayer, like sex, is the most intimate of connections with another. To confess our need of prayer and our fear of such vulnerability makes it far more possible to enter into meaningful conversation with each other and God.

RESOURCES FOR REFERRAL

A good leader knows her limitations. It is not necessary for us as leaders to be able to offer all the help a person may need, as long as we have some idea who might. Help may come in the form of a book or the name of a good therapist. Help may come from someone in the church or the broader community who has passed through the same struggle. There is no need for anyone to struggle alone and without information.

The ability to make referrals requires simply being open to the role of community in addressing the complexity of life. For example, to whom would you turn if you learn that a man in your group is struggling with pornography? What would you do if you found out that a woman is suffering bouts of depression related to past sexual abuse? A couple may be in the middle of menopause and not even know its symptoms or the complications it can mean for a marriage. There will always be more to know than we can possibly learn, but someone in our church, neighborhood or community knows how to help. How do we find them?

An Intimate Marriage leader needs to start a help file. A great place to begin is with your pastor. To whom do they refer marriage problems? To whom do they refer for help with depression, sexual abuse and sexual addiction? It is always important to find out from others who have used the services of professional helpers whom they would recommend.

An Intimate Marriage group leader will sometimes hear from a person through e-mail, a phone call or a lunch appointment that more is going on in that person's marriage than meets the eye. It is important then to give room for conversation. A friend told me of a phone call from a member of his group who said he was looking for a book on sexual addiction. It would have been easy to say either "I don't know" or "I've heard *False Intimacy* is a good book." *False Intimacy* by Harry Schaumburg is indeed an excellent book, but it is a mistake to offer a book without engaging the one asking for the resource. My friend did a courageous and simple thing. He asked the man, "I have a good resource, but do you mind if I ask if it is for you or someone else?"

The man hesitated and finally said, "It's for me. This group has stirred up some things in me that I've got to face."

My friend then said, "If you'd like to meet to pray and talk, I'd be glad to do so. But I also know some folks in our church who meet weekly to talk about matters of sexual struggle. I don't want to rush you, but I want you to know there are resources if and when you want to use them."

Our task as leaders is to shepherd those in our group. If a person expresses a concern, we simply need to point toward hope, make connections and then follow up. A leader can't make a person change or seek other help, but sometimes a phone call a few days after a suggestion has been made can clinch the connection. "Hey John, I'm calling to tell you I've been praying. I wonder if you've had a chance to make a call to the therapist I recommended." Even a phone message is a kind way to say, "The Hound of Heaven is nipping at your heels."

LOVE OF REDEMPTION

Group leaders must love the way God has nipped at their heels and wooed them back to himself. The goal of this study series is to build strong marriages, but even more to allow our marriages to draw and drive us to God. The more joy we know in our marriage, the more our heart will be seized with gratitude. The more havoc we experience in our marriage, the more we will be driven in desperation to the only One who can truly nourish us. Whether we are in peace or at war, we will know joy only in the wonder of redemption. A leader must love redemption because he has seen its fruit in his life and marriage.

A love of redemption is based on the confidence of faith and the imagination of hope. We can offer only what we have known to be true in our own life. In that sense we can never take anyone any further than we have gone. If our faith is merely book-true, then we will offer others little more than the facts of redemption. If we have stories of redemption that give credence to the truths of the Bible, however, we will not be dismayed by the complex stories that unfold so slowly before us. We will wait patiently and groan with those who suffer. Our ability to sensitively enter stories of suffering is directly proportional to our confidence in the promise of God's provision.

Whether we are in peace or at war, we will know joy only in the wonder of redemption.

One of the greatest gifts we give to those in our group is the hope that God redeems. There is no heartache too deep, no sin too egregious for God's ability to heal. Therefore hope doesn't need to be tied to a particular technique, book or guru. God can work through our watching a movie, reading a book or listening to a song. What awakens the heart? What rouses conscience? Who can call forth a spirit dead to hope? No one can transform a heart but the Spirit of God. Consequently, a good leader simply stirs the pot of redemption and calls forth God to work.

This doesn't lessen our work or the importance of our preparation. Instead, it relieves us of the necessity to figure out how to make redemption happen. If we simply recall how God has rescued us from one of many catastrophes, it becomes apparent there is little rhyme or reason to his mercy, beyond his sovereign pleasure to bestow grace when and where he wishes.

A good leader moves into problems and complexity aware of his or her limits, open to the promise of God's arrival and confident that in due season God's kindness will alter the hearts of those who seek him.

STARTING THE JOURNEY

The decision has been made, and perhaps the launch date has been set. There is no turning back. You are going to lead a marriage group.

Think of leading the group like taking an adventure trip to Costa Rica. The country is exotic and foreign to all your previous experiences. You would never simply buy a ticket and take off. You would do research to find out about the country before you got there. You'd purchase travel guides, do Internet searches and, if possible, talk to people who have lived in or visited Costa Rica. It should be no different with running a group. Become as familiar as you can with the unfamiliar before you actually get there.

This guide will serve as an excellent introduction, but the more you learn, the more questions you will want answered. After leading your first group meeting, you will need to reread some of this leader's guide in order to make use of your mistakes and prepare for your next experience. You might also want to look for a full-length book on small groups such as Jeff Arnold's *The Big Book on Small Groups.* Leading groups is a skill that will grow over a lifetime once it gets in your blood.

The more you learn,

the more questions you

will want answered.

This chapter will take you from the decision to start a group through your first meeting. The next chapter will help you reflect on the stages of group life and the complexities that may arise.

All the suggestions offered here are open to modification or outright reversal. There are no immutable laws for running a group, though some principles like defining group goals and norms and maintaining confidentiality are so important that it would be foolhardy to ignore them. Your group will reflect your style and philosophy of learning and relationships. Our goal is simply to get you thinking about crucial elements of running a group.

SELECTION OF MEMBERS

A key question to be asked is, how many couples will be in the group and who will those couples be? There are no magical numbers or exact research to indicate the perfect number. However, the greater the number, the more complex and impersonal the process will be. A group with more than six couples (including you) is unwieldy, and a group with only three couples is too small. It is likely best to have a group with no fewer than eight and no more than twelve members, or four to six couples.

Sometimes members are assigned to groups by church leaders or formed on the basis of sign-ups. There is nothing wrong with this selection process. Often the gain is diversity and opportunities to meet new people. The disadvantage is the likelihood of some initial awkwardness and the need for a longer period to develop rapport and trust.

Selection can also be done on the basis of prior knowledge of the couples, perhaps through a neighborhood group or some affinity. Homogenous affinity groups (according to age, years married, stage of life, sociological similarity) have the advantage of a similar set of life concerns, which means greater ease in initially forming relationships. The disadvantage is the likelihood of "groupthink" or peer pressure. Over time, members of groups with less diversity tend to be more concerned about their status or how they appear to others in the group. Obviously, there are advantages and disadvantages to all choices.

Once a group has formed or the decision has been made to ask members to be in a group, the leader needs to explain to each person or couple what membership in the group will mean. This is perhaps one of the most important but least utilized components of group work. It is crucial to talk to each couple before the first group at least once; I'd recommend at least twice.

INVITATION OR CONFIRMATION

"John, this is Randy. Hey, how are you? I am calling to ask if you and Helen would like to be in a small group at church that will be studying the topic of marriage."

"John, this is Randy. Hey, how are you? I am calling to confirm your involvement with us in the small group study on marriage."

Once the initial invitation or confirmation has been made, a whole host of details regarding the time, place, materials and other members of the group need to be addressed.

But it is not enough to offer only technical details about the group in the phone call. Three important elements ought to be covered:

- group goals and responsibilities
- risks and rewards
- group norms and processes

It is not crucial to cover these in exhaustive detail, but it's wise to get the basics out on the table at the beginning. Then the same issues will be discussed in greater detail at the first formal gathering.

Group Goals and Responsibilities

You can make the group as free-wheeling and unstructured or as regimented as you wish. It is imperative to set the length of time the group will meet before the first meeting. In any case, group members have every right to know beforehand what is expected of them.

If I were expressing the goals of the group, I'd say, "This group is designed to address the foundation of what makes a marriage work. In Genesis 2 God tells us to leave our mother and father, weave intimacy and cleave to one another by becoming one flesh. This study will address what it means to leave, weave and cleave. It will also give us each opportunities to talk about our particular successes and failures and how we can grow in our marriage. God willing, an additional benefit will be the involvement of caring for several other couples who are facing some of the same struggles and challenges."

> *It is a Bible study,*
>
> *not a therapeutic*
>
> *intervention.*

I'd add that the group is not designed to provide group therapy or to be the place to divulge one's deepest struggles and hurts in marriage. It is a Bible study, not a therapeutic intervention. But I'd say quite clearly, "As group leaders, my wife and I will be talking honestly about our struggles in order to illustrate the material, and we would invite you to do the same if it helps us better understand the material we will be studying."

The responsibilities of a member couple are threefold.

- Don't miss group meetings. Make sure your calendar is free from the get-go.
- Don't be late. (It is wise, though, to allow the first portion of each meeting to be a social, snacking, catch-up time to make sure everyone is present for the beginning of the formal study.)

- Be prepared. It is pointless to show up without having done the work. (You should let people know that the Bible study will require an hour of preparation time *and* at least an hour of conversation with one's spouse before each group meeting. Car-time conversations don't count. Talk time needs to be put into the calendar, with no competition from children, phone calls or other distractions.)

If those three commitments can't be made, a couple should not agree to be in the group. In the long run, the least committed couple will often determine the outcome for the entire group. That means prospective participants must make sure a basic commitment to their marriage is strong enough to warrant their being in the group.

Risks and Rewards

Help couples count the cost before joining the group. This is best done briefly, often by recommending the couple read Luke 14 and pray. I'd recommend saying, "John and Carol, we are so thrilled you've agreed to be part of the group. We know that all marriages are under some kind of stress and challenge; more accurately said, we are all under some kind of assault. Evil simply doesn't want our marriage to succeed.

"As we enter this study, I encourage the two of you to consider what you'd most like to work on in your marriage. The studies are designed to help us all more honestly look at our weaknesses and be grateful for our strengths. If there are no challenges in your marriage, then there really isn't much reason to attend. But given how difficult it is, at least for me, to be honest about my weaknesses, I'd encourage the two of you to talk, pray and prepare for a pretty exciting roller-coaster ride as we step into this study together."

The couple may wish to ask questions. Be prepared to tell a few stories about what you've begun to address with your spouse in preparation for the study.

Group Norms and Processes

Most people will not think to ask how the group will be run. But it will likely build confidence in you as a group leader to address a few concerns before they arise. I suggest that you address the issues of confidentiality, subgrouping, boundaries and conflict.

- Confidentiality: Each member of the group needs to know what confidentiality means. Don't presume it is understood. Confidentiality means that everything of a personal nature that is discussed remains in the group. Nothing that any participant reveals about their marriage, their partner, themselves or anyone else can be communicated outside the group to anyone who is not part of the group.
- Subgrouping: Group members must commit themselves to avoid talking about fellow members and their marriages outside the group, unless all parties agree that the

matter will be discussed when the group reconvenes. Say two group participants meet for coffee and another participant becomes their subject of discussion. Is that legitimate? It is not honorable unless the two promise that everything they say will be later expressed to the person or couple not present. This is the only way to keep members from indulging in group gossip, which would be as great a violation of trust as breaking confidentiality.

- Boundaries: There is always a tension between self-disclosure and propriety. In most groups individual self-disclosure doesn't implicate one's spouse, but in a marriage group to name an individual struggle brings one's spouse into the discussion. It would be pointless to run a marriage group that didn't address real problems and struggles, but addressing real problems requires great sensitivity. All self-disclosure must be vetted by one's spouse before it is spoken in the group. A group norm is that no issue can be brought up in the group can occur before it has been discussed by the couple alone.

- Conflict: Tensions in a marriage or a group are necessary for growth. This needs to be said a number of times and discussed by the group. If tension is not allowed to be expressed, it will simply come to the surface in subtle and disingenuous ways. How a leader and a group addresses conflict will determine the profitability of the group. No tension makes a group sterile and boring, yet too much tension makes a group terrifying and defensive. A core set of boundaries will allow no contempt, no blaming, no accusations and no hostile silence or retreating. Conflict resolution is not the goal of the group, nor is resolution of long-term problems. The group ought not to descend into hearing each partner's complaint and then trying to come up with a reasonable or biblical way to resolve the problem. Not only would such a group fail to attend to the study, but seldom if ever would its input resolve a couple's long-standing issues. Such airing of grievances would inevitably alienate and frustrate the group. We will address how to confront conflict in the next chapter, but a boundary issue needs to be first established. The boundary involves the stated expectation that *the group is not into problem solving, referring conflicts or making judgments of right or wrong.*

> **Tensions in a marriage**
>
> **or a group are**
>
> **necessary for growth.**

Once these issues are laid out for a participating couple, it is wise to say, "Let me call you back in a couple days to see if there are any questions or concerns that I can address before the group begins." A second phone call will help clarify and sweep away any anxieties that may have arisen in the wake of the first phone call. Most often, this second phone call will take little time, but such a process allows the first group meeting to go far more smoothly.

FIRST MEETING

The first meeting ought to accomplish two things: restatement of the expectations, norms and goals of the study group and beginning to get to know each other. It may seem redundant, but you'll do well to go over everything you covered in the initial phone call. Likely you've heard some common questions from all the couples, and it is wise to write those questions down and address them.

I'd want to hear from each couple what they hope will happen for them as individuals and as a couple through the study process. This helps personalize their goals. Don't expect this discussion to be too long or too personal. You'll do well to ask as well, "What concerns do you have about being in a marriage group?" The answers will likely be generic but more revealing.

Then move into a more significant time of introduction. Nearly every couple has a well-established story of how they met, courted, came into conflict, made up and got married. Having each couple bring and show either their wedding album or a few favorite wedding pictures is a fabulous way to get people telling their story.

In the first meeting participants should hear something about the unique dimensions of one another's marriage. Pictures and details of first meetings and courtship are easy to show and tell and yet are highly revelatory of some of the strengths and weaknesses of one's marriage. Couples will feel far more invested in one another, more curious and open to each other, if they share formative stories with one another. Divide the time equally, and make sure each couple uses all their time before the next couple takes their turn.

At the end of the first evening, the group leader can summarize some of the common themes and struggles that are represented in the group. Plans for the next meeting can be established, and by this point it will be a natural and bonding experience to pray. If there is time left over, you can laugh about the wedding pictures of those married in the 1970s—a uniquely tragic era that misused ruffles and the colors brown and orange, and mixed it all with thick sideburns, longish hair and sentimental songs.

SUBSEQUENT MEETINGS

Nothing serves a group better than a good beginning. Some groups set up social events as adjuncts to the study; other groups don't attempt to mix outside the formal meeting time. In either case, a slow, well-orchestrated beginning will build confidence in the leader and ease in participating in the group.

Beginning with the second meeting, jump into the formal study. How the group is run will involve an interplay between the leader's initial form and the group's response. It is ridiculous to be autocratic and run the group like a drill team. On the other hand, the group needs a point person to start the process to help them craft the kind of group experience that best serves their goals. Some groups will be highly interactive; others will be more comfortable staying on task. There is no "right" way to run a group, other than to make sure there is both movement through the material and plenty of opportunity for everyone to speak.

After several meetings, it makes sense to spend a portion of an evening getting feedback on how each person is experiencing the group. You might say, "Before we end tonight I want us each to reflect on whether the group is moving in a direction that is helpful and consistent with what you had hoped. Before we are done, let's consider what midcourse revisions we may need to make to ensure that the group is a profitable experience for you." Not every suggestion can be implemented, but the group can be called to form a clearer sense of what is possible and desirable.

TOWARD THE END OF THE STUDY

As a leader you ought to know your level of commitment to the group beyond the initial study. If you have signed on for only one Bible study lasting six or seven weeks, that should be stated from the beginning. If you are open to leading the group through a series of studies, it may be wise to wait until you've passed through the third or fourth week before addressing the possibility of a longer commitment.

Every group will need to answer the question of duration. This series includes seven study guides with six separate studies in each, for a total of forty-two weeks. The material is built on the three-part command to leave, weave and cleave. Each of these core elements of marriage is the focus of at least one Bible study guide. If I were to lead an Intimate Marriage Bible study, I'd start by using the first booklet, *The Goal of Marriage*. If there were a commitment to do only one other study, I'd recommend moving directly to the *Forgiveness* study, which takes up sin, repentance, forgiveness and reconciliation.

Let me express our hope: the ideal is to do all seven study guides in the course of a year. If that choice is made, then we would recommend that everyone in the group first read our book *The Intimate Mystery*. Then your group can begin Bible study with *The Goal of Marriage*, on leaving, weaving and cleaving.

If you begin in mid-September, this will take you through the first or second week of

November. Most groups will not sustain study through the Thanksgiving-Christmas holiday season. For many couples, however, it is advisable to obtain the second study guide, *Family Ties,* before the holidays begin. Holidays are significant points of family enmeshment, disappointment and pressure. To have the study guide in hand before the holidays with full knowledge that the topic will be addressed in early January will allow the material to ferment into a rich brew.

[Leaving] is one of the least understood and least lived-out commands in the Bible.

The *Family Ties* studies will help couples talk about the issues of leaving. You can be assured this will bring up significant struggle for many couples. It is one of the least understood and least lived-out commands in the Bible. Consequently, it is wise to follow this study up with *Communication,* which is directly related to weaving. Following that material, it is wise not to move on to sexuality but to study *Male and Female,* taking up issues related to the differences between male and female; these will tie directly to the issues of communication.

Next we recommend that your group step into the *Forgiveness* study guide. This will be a watershed set of studies, due to the hard work done prior. If it had been taken up earlier in the process, the group's treatment would have been far more predictable and facile.

If the couples in the group have been willing to engage these issues and have grown in their capacity to honor each other and seek forgiveness, then you'll do well to continue with the last two studies. Entering the turbulent and glorious waters of sexuality with the *Sexual Intimacy* guide is now appropriate. To do so earlier, without a strong foundation, would be risky. To save sexuality for the very last set of studies wouldn't provide a sufficient buffer for more reflection.

As the final set of studies, we recommend *Dreams & Demands,* which takes up various complex issues that arise in most marriages. This is a great way to return to the core material and reinforce the three-legged foundation of a successful marriage.

EMBRACING CHAOS, CONFLICT AND CHANGE

It takes courage to lead. Or it takes foolishness to lead and courage to remain in the fray once the shooting starts. And the shooting will come—be assured of that.

What you are doing will matter for eternity. You are inviting couples to take seriously their vows, deepen their bond and confront sin in themselves, their spouse and their culture. You are taking on evil in an area it is deeply committed to destroy. Don't be surprised by the level of chaos and conflict, nor by the passionate heart of God, who is more committed to marriage than we can ever be. He desires change, and he intends to bring transformation to the heart of each person in your group. If there is no chaos and conflict, there will not be deep change. If we expect chaos and conflict, we can be better prepared to deal with it.

What you are doing

will matter for eternity.

Heed this warning. There are no techniques or simple steps for handling the complexities of a group, let alone life. But we can develop wisdom and get a perspective on the terrain we are to walk even if we can't detail the exact steps to take. Many complexities may arise in your group beyond those we address here, but after a while you will see that most other issues are subvarieties of the ones we cover.

LATECOMERS AND NO-SHOWS

There are three kinds of latecomers: inadvertent, avoidant and passive-aggressive. The inadvertent latecomer ran into heavy traffic, got a last-minute phone call or just lost track of the time. It is not a pattern, and the late arrival will likely be addressed the moment they arrive with either an apology or an explanation. Not much needs to be done but to smile and remember the many times you have missed a deadline or a meeting.

The avoidant latecomer is likely ambivalent about being at the group. Their tardiness will be fairly regular and often becomes an issue early on. There will be a handful of excuses, but as their tardiness proves to be regular it almost seems they want to be asked to stop attending. Typically these people are not late to other meetings, nor do they seem irresponsible in other areas of life. It may be that one spouse is ready and willing to be on time but the other dallies and creates tension prior to coming. If this is not the person's general pattern, then it is likely associated with fear regarding what might be exposed about their marriage.

The best way to handle the avoidant latecomer is to ask after a few absences or tardy entries if there is some reluctance to be in the group. Most of the time, the answer will be a polite no. Press on. You can ask directly whether the tardiness might be related to some concerns or fears about being in the group, given that they are seldom late to other events. Even if nothing comes of the discussion, it will likely cure the tardiness and help the couple to name their struggles in private.

The passive-aggressive latecomer is maddening. This is a person whose style of relating is to put people on the defensive by consistent tardiness. Over time his or her lateness may become a joke, but the thin humor is a veneer covering disrespect and violence. Passive-aggressive lateness makes everyone wait. Making others wait is a power move. If people wait, then the latecomer is king. If people start without him, then others must either catch him up (king) or ignore him (pauper). In either case, he is in control. In one sense, it doesn't matter if he is the king or the pauper because he has caused others in the group to feel powerless and defensive. He has disrupted the group, and that gives him power.

This form of tardiness is deeply set in one's character, and the person's spouse may well have learned to cover it over and provide ample excuses for the repeated lateness. Amazingly, the passive-aggressive latecomer seldom apologizes; if he does, his words seem perfunctory and hollow.

There is little to do in this case but to ask the couple to reconsider their participation in the group. The one who is passive-aggressive will be offended and defensive; the innocent but rescuing spouse will be horrified and promise to be on time henceforth. It is best to say, "Folks, if I understand you both correctly, the lateness is not unique to your participation in this group but is a significant pattern in your marriage. If so, then I doubt we can hope for it to change by mere will or choice. Instead, I'd like to ask you two to consider talking with a therapist who might be able to help you see how this has become a pattern in your life and marriage. We'd love to have you remain in the group, but not at the expense of the other members' commitments to be here and to be on time. What would you both be willing to do about this pattern?"

MONOPOLIZING CONVERSATION

Nearly every community or group has at least one know-it-all. For most people the term is a slam, but to the know-it-all it is a compliment. Often this person is very bright and knows a great deal. What they lack is a high enough E.Q.—emotional intelligence quotient—to read how others perceive their dogged monopolizing of the conversation.

Often two kinds of intervention are needed—a public reminder of the rules of the road and a more private interaction to solidify the group norm. After the talkative member finishes, it is useful to ask if others have a different view or, if similar, how they would put the matter in their own words. In most cases, the talkative one will soon want to step back in to debate or clarify her or his position. At that point a kind yet firm remark needs to be made: "John, your views are important to us all, but when you state your position so vocally, it makes it difficult for others to feel as free to offer their perspective. Please make sure you are leaving room for everyone to have a voice."

It is usually wise to follow up an interaction like this with a phone call to check in. See if the monopolizing member is aware of the pattern and open to asking the big question: *what does my monopolizing tell me about myself?* If the person is open to thinking about that question, then it is a simple step to ask, "What do you think the effect of that pattern is on your spouse?" This may be one of the kindest gifts the monopolizer and his or her spouse may ever have received.

SUPERFICIALITY

No one ought to feel pressured to be honest. We are all at different points of growth and willingness to risk, and there should not be a base level of disclosure that is required. But some members of your group will go well beyond not sharing to glossing over problems with a veneer of shellac: "Well, Steve and I used to struggle until I realized that I just need to turn lemons into lemonade."

What can be said to such a gloss? Not much other than a stiff, uncomfortable smile and an awkward reentry into reality. Such superficiality is a conversation stopper. It is tough to go through such shellac, and it is hard to get around it.

One way to avoid the potholes of superficiality is to remind one another that marriage, like life, has no answers, only a Person whom we are called to trust—Jesus. The answers we find are at best tentative and incomplete, but we can lean absolutely on him.

If the pattern of superficiality persists through most of the group member's interactions, then it may become necessary to simply disagree with that approach to life. The leader needs to bless the person's resolve to find solace in the midst of a confusing and disturbing world, without requiring the rest of the group to be bogged down by such dogged cheeriness.

Marriage, like life, has no answers, only a Person whom we are called to trust—Jesus. The answers we find are at best tentative and incomplete, but we can lean absolutely on him.

TOO REVEALING

The opposite of superficiality is not depth but wanton exposure. The revealer seems to relish the opportunity to go further, say more or discuss in greater detail matters that are often left private. This is not a matter of honesty; it is habitual inappropriateness.

This person loves to say, "I just tell it like it is." They may defend themselves by adding, "Look, if you can't handle the truth, then that's your problem, not mine." The revealer usually majors on secrets, sexual struggles or misadventures, and matters of shame. There is a barely hidden, or sometimes quite obvious, pleasure in shocking others.

Usually such a pattern needs to be addressed quickly in the group. If it is avoided, the revealer will just up the ante. The leader can say, "Jill, I suspect you know that you are unnerving some in the group by your frank language and description. Is that your purpose? And if not, then would you consider how you want to approach matters that need to be addressed with more propriety?"

If the inappropriate disclosures continue, it is likely the person simply has never heard others explain the effect such words have on them. What is important to define for the person and the group is what constitutes a disclosure that goes beyond what is normally shared and takes people into details or scenes that cannot be described without a compromise of integrity.

CONFLICT IN THE GROUP

Conflict comes from tension that arises as well-entrenched defenses are challenged. We each live with well-defended paradigms of ourselves, our marriage, God and life, and usually we are not grateful when someone begins to shake our foundations. But paradigm shifts are necessary for growth and transformation. A group leader must expect and anticipate conflict.

The goal is not so much to minimize conflict as to prepare group members for it. More often than not, some form of disagreement will arise. For many, any public disagreement is frightening. The group leader needs to honor the disagreement, thank the participants and glory in the norm of "agreeing to disagree." Once conflict is seen not to be disruptive enough to derail the group, most members will relax.

Some conflict can't be honored and embraced. When a couple begins to fight in the group, the leader must step in quickly, with no hesitation. It is similar to sailing on a mountain lake. Winds can whistle down a mountain at the speed of an arrow. When the water begins to ripple and trees begin to shake, sailors must not hesitate. The sails must be either reefed rapidly or brought down; otherwise the boat is apt to be slammed on its side.

Conflict can draw a group into complex issues with high energy and commitment, or it can wither a group's resolve with the acidic power of contempt.

The group leader can say, "Marcy and Tony, obviously this is a contentious issue for you both. No doubt, since the turbulence surfaced so rapidly, it is not a new issue. We'd love to be of help, but that can't happen in this group if we let you two go at it. How would you like us to be part? We can't be your referees or your judge. What would you like from us?"

The leader has stopped the conflict by naming it. He has contextualized the disagreement, implying that it is not a new issue, and then he has invited the couple to ask for help within the limits of what the group can do.

Conflict can be intense and creative, but too often

it devolves into some form of contempt, blame or accusation. Conflict can draw a group into complex issues with high energy and commitment, or it can wither a group's resolve with the acidic power of contempt. The group leader is responsible to discern the difference. Contempt belittles and demeans; creative conflict involves argument within a mood of collaboration and encouragement. The difference is difficult to describe in print, but in operation it is as obvious as the nose on the other's face.

What is difficult to describe is the rise of the eyebrow, the scrunching up of the face, the shrug of the shoulders or the other embodiments of contempt. Invective, accusation and blame are not difficult to discern, but contempt can be insidious. Even a slight curl of the lip can squelch the momentum of a group.

Contempt is a wicked tool to regain power or punish someone who has hurt you. Often the person who uses contempt feels that they are on the verge of giving up hope or have already surrendered to despair. Contempt is a desperate attack that doesn't seek redress or reconciliation, just "an eye for an eye." For that reason most people intuitively know to keep out of the way—but the group leader must not surrender to this impulse.

In an Intimate Marriage group it is important to name your own fear. "Sylvia, your words are so strong and so full of hurt and anger that I find myself afraid to even stop you." The expression of fear may help the person who is blaming or accusing the other with contempt to step out of the cycle long enough to see themselves with the eyes of the other. This can break the cycle.

Once the cycle is broken, however, likely the blamer will either stonewall and go silent with more contempt or slide away in dissociation because of shame. In the first case, the blamer will pout. In the case of dissociation, you will sense that the person is no longer with you. It is as if they have disappeared. When someone is stonewalling, you feel as if you're being dared to interact. When the person is dissociating, it's like seeing the other person fade away to nothingness.

Now the true drama begins. If the blamer is stonewalling, it is nearly impossible to simply return to the study. That would feel disingenuous and cowardly. But to linger and invite the blamer to talk is like trying to negotiate with a hostage taker. The person's speeches are long and convoluted. What can be done?

First see if the blamer is interested in thinking the issue through from the "log in your eye first" perspective. Of course this involves a big risk. Most blamers will not want to do so; they will either sulk or walk out. In either case, the next step is to ask the group what they would like to do: "Folks, we are in the middle of a meltdown. If we try to proceed, we will feel like we are avoiding a huge elephant in the living room. If we pursue Meg at this point, we'll be stymied, because she seems not to want to look at her part first. We're in a bind. What direction would you like to take?"

It is not a failure of leadership to turn this decision over to the group. It would be weakness to avoid naming the bind and arrogance to think you can decide for the group how to handle it. Of course when you present the decision to the group, anxiety will rise. They have merely watched the meltdown, and now you are inviting them to join it. Expect silence. Expect tension. Process that and allow the group to choose how it wants to continue.

Through this experience the group will learn that contempt has no place in a group or a marriage and that its resolution comes not through avoidance but by direct, kind exposure. When a disruption this large occurs in a group, make sure it is addressed first at the next group meeting. Otherwise it will turn into a monstrous elephant that will impede all future progress. The group will also learn that even ugly failures of love need not derail the work of God. Most everyone will be able to identify moments like this in their marriage that were not handled well and served to create a DMZ (demilitarized zone) and shut down progress.

Be aware that the aftermath for the leader will be a dark night of the soul. There will be countless questions about whether it could have been handled better. The answer is that of course it could, but self-incrimination and severe self-doubt are not called for. A good leader ponders failures only to the point of considering what might be done better next time, not to punish herself for real or perceived mistakes.

PROMISCUITY, PORNOGRAPHY, ABUSE AND SHAME

We are sexual beings and we sin. We all sin sexually. Since the Fall, our physical nakedness and our sexuality have been suffused in shame. These are tough issues and will require enormous prayer and care as they are approached in the group. Such issues will likely come to the surface in the study on sexuality, though they can arise at any moment in connection with any topic. They are like an infection that can suddenly spring up and, if left untreated, can destroy.

One dilemma is that we have not developed language or customs for naming these struggles. For many in the group, any confession of sexual struggle will already feel like an inappropriate disclosure. It is not, but the group leader will need to step in quickly and check on whether the matter has already been talked over with the discloser's spouse: "Mike, thank you for your honesty, but before you continue to speak, we need to make sure you've already talked to Diane and have her permission to bring this up in the group." If the answer is no, then a group norm must be honored and the discussion tabled until the two talk outside of the group.

If permission has been granted, a second issue surfaces. The group is not a replacement for counseling; therefore the question must be posed: "Mike, you know we can't do therapy here. So what would be helpful?" If Mike is illustrating a point or asking for prayer and accountability, then the group should be able to help. If he is looking for absolution or a safe place to tell his spouse, then the group is being misused.

When sexual struggles are talked about, it is important to focus on what the group can provide rather than attempting to resolve the problems being discussed. With any long-term personal battle, little can be said in the short run to alter the struggle. It is a significant mistake to criticize or remind the person that sexual sin is damaging or against God's will. Even the best-intentioned counsel or advice comes across as hollow and minimizes the immensity of the battle.

We are sexual beings

and we sin.

We all sin sexually.

It is far better to ask if the person is in a group for sexual addiction or seeing a therapist who specializes in such issues. If not, then it is possible to ask a simple question: "When will you seek help, and what has kept you from doing so up to this point?"

When the struggles have to do with the shame of past sexual abuse, both husband and wife are in need of information about the issues of abuse.[1] Both partners in a marriage affected by sexual abuse will profit from personal and marital counseling. Counseling will help them break through the barriers and experience relational and sexual intimacy without the struggles of shame. The group can offer stories from their own experience and can support the couple to seek healing and remain faithful to the process.

When sexual struggles are disclosed, the group's proper response is to honor the couple's courage and provide a context in which their heartache can be heard and brought before God. Once the issues are out on the table, the most delicate and difficult dance will need to be engaged.

Remember this truth: *Difficult issues can be disclosed with only a modicum of shame, but as soon as the discloser leaves the meeting, shame will hit with hurricane force. In the next interaction with that person, shame will be a barrier to relationship.*

Once highly personal matters have been discussed, the leader must manage the experience of shame for the individual, the couple and the group. This requires a few phone calls to both partners before the next meeting. It is best to jump directly into the

---

[1]Dan B. Allender, *The Wounded Heart* (Colorado Springs: NavPress, 1990).

issue of shame: "Jan, I know it was not easy to tell us what you did, and if you are anything like me, the last few days have probably been hell for you. I really want to thank you for your honesty, and I pray you've not turned against yourself, or Seth, or the group to cover your shame. How are you? And please don't tell me you're fine."

When the group reconvenes, it is wise to readdress the things that were stirred up by the person's confession. Don't be surprised if others begin to come clean about some of the struggles they've hidden from view. The same process can begin as other couples start to name their struggles.

ADVICE GIVING, SELF-RIGHTEOUSNESS AND PATRONIZATION

One of the most difficult practices to guard against is the pervasive pattern of advice giving. It seems so Christian and caring to offer suggestions, advice and counsel to those whose struggles seem similar to our own. We live in a knowledge jungle, with a glut of information and a thousand gurus to help resolve any and every human struggle.

To the degree we are advice ready, we are curiosity slow. Hearing only the tip of a problem, we rush to offer our solutions. The Bible tells us to be slow to speak, slow to anger and ready to listen. This is particularly important when someone begins to tell us their problems. Even if they want help or demand specific steps to resolve their heartache, it is a mistake to pander to that longing with cheap advice.

> *To the degree we are advice ready, we are curiosity slow.*

It must become a group norm to listen and not offer counsel. Does this make it impossible to suggest a book or a therapist or a helpful support group? I hope not, but it should sensitize each member to enter into conversation with others in a way that models what the group leader hopes will occur in each marriage. We are modeling a new way of living, and what you want in a marriage should happen in the group.

Especially destructive is counsel that comes with an air of patronizing self-righteousness. This benevolence is sickeningly sweet and sincere and will likely make group members' skin crawl. It is enormously difficult to challenge in the group; however, the group leader can ask the person receiving the counsel, "When Jonathan was offering his ideas, I noticed it was hard for you to look him in the face. Can you tell us, Jack, what you were feeling?"

Likely there will not be a full-fledged disclosure, but there may be enough for the leader to then add, "Jonathan, I know you want to help, and no doubt you believe you were offering help with the best of intentions, but if I were Jack I'd have felt like you were treating me like a ten-year-old."

There may be defensiveness or protestations of innocence and well-meaning care, but the harm has been mitigated. The leader can further the conversation at that point by saying, "Jonathan, I'd be glad to meet with you sometime this week to clarify what I'm trying to tell you and to hear out what you wanted Jack to hear." The issues are likely best addressed in an individual interaction once the pattern has been exposed.

No one can predict what will transpire in a group, but it is reasonable to expect the wild, woolly and unreasonable. The marriage group's momentous potential for transformation makes chaos a certainty. What is required is less a mastery of the complexity than a willingness to jump into the fray with the armaments of prayer, humility and openness. God's work is greater than evil's intentions, and faithfulness in spite of our fears and ignorance is all that God desires for us to offer and all he needs for profound change to occur.

BIBLE STUDY
THEME OVERVIEW

This chapter's overview of the content of each of the Bible study guides in the Intimate Marriage Series is intended to better equip you to take a small group or a church community through the material.

THE GOAL OF MARRIAGE

God provides the foundation for marriage in his command to Adam to *leave* his parents, *weave* a new life with his wife and *cleave* together in sexual intimacy.

Topics and Passages

Study 1: Knowing Who We Are as Husband and Wife (Genesis 1:26-31; 2:7)

Study 2: Leaving—from the Male Perspective (Genesis 2)

Study 3: Leaving—from the Female Perspective (Psalm 45:10-15)

Study 4: Weaving (Ecclesiastes 4:7-12)

Study 5: Cleaving (Genesis 2:18-25)

Study 6: The Ultimate Loyalty (Psalm 127)

Key Points

1. It is important to understand who we are as human beings in order to understand both our spouse and the very institution of marriage.
2. Human beings are created in the image of God and reflect the glory of their Creator.
3. Human beings are sinners who in rebellion have fractured their relationship with God and consequently with their fellow human beings.

4. Marriage thus brings together two glorious image breakers and two fundamentally selfish sinners.

5. God established marriage in order to dispel human loneliness.

6. Genesis 2:24 presents the divine imperative for a successful marriage: a man *leaves* his parents (Psalm 45 puts this in terms of the woman) and *weaves* a life with his wife, and they *cleave* in sexual union.

7. The most important foundation for a strong marriage is a vibrant relationship with God.

Synopsis

The Goal of Marriage is foundational to all the other studies. It is possible to benefit from using one of the other six study guides in the series without having worked through this one, but we believe that your study of the later guides will be all the richer and more effective if this guide is used as early as possible in your group.

The first study explores who we are as a husband and a wife according to the creation account in Genesis 1—2. In particular, it reflects on the fact that men and women are created in the image of God. Most important, at least as regards the marriage relationship, we learn that our creation in God's image means that we reflect his glory. It is a derivative glory, just as the moon's light is a reflection of the sun's, but the implications for marriage are tremendous. This study calls on participants to meditate on what it means for marriage that their spouse is an image-bearing creature.

> *Marriage . . . brings together two glorious image breakers and two fundamentally selfish sinners.*

The next few studies (2-5) are based on the divine pronouncement in Genesis 2:24 that marriage involves leaving, weaving and cleaving. Study two looks at what it means for a man to leave his parents to be married. After ruling out the requirement that leaving be a physical abandonment, we come to realize that what is at issue is the creation of a new primary loyalty. No longer is the man's primary loyalty to his parents; it is now directed toward his new wife. Boundaries need to be established so the new relationship can be nurtured and grow in trust and confidence. Upon further thought, we realize that it is not only our loyalty to parents that needs to be modified but also our loyalties to other things and people in our past.

Psalm 45, the passage being discussed in study three, calls on a bride to leave her past loyalties as well and form a new primary alliance with her husband. Women face different issues from those men typically confront at such a transitional moment, so study three seeks to uncover them.

In marriage a man and a woman are called not just to leave but to form a new relationship. This involves weaving two separate lives into one. Study four takes a look at Ecclesiastes 4, a passage that extols the advantages of relationship in a difficult, problempacked world. What is true for relationship in general is certainly true of the most intense and intimate of human relationships, marriage. In a preliminary way, since a later study guide is devoted entirely to the subject, study four introduces the importance of good communication for the weaving together of two lives.

In the next study the focus returns again to Genesis 2, but this time a new topic is under review: the climactic cleaving of two people into one. Again, a later study guide will be entirely devoted to this topic, sexuality.

Psalm 127 is the center of the final discussion. Here we see that while wife and husband must make their relationship primary among all their other relationships here on earth, their individual and corporate relationship with God is the bedrock on which it must be built.

Further Resources

These studies are from three biblical books: Genesis, Psalms and Ecclesiastes. The following commentaries are highly recommended for those who want to study the passages more carefully.

Allen, L. C. *Psalms 101–150.* Word Biblical Commentary. Waco, Tex.: Word, 1983.

Longman, Tremper, III. *Ecclesiastes.* New International Commentary on the Old Testament. Grand Rapids, Mich.: Eerdmans, 1997.

Provan, Iain. *Ecclesiastes, Song of Songs.* NIV Application Commentary. Grand Rapids, Mich.: Zondervan, 2001.

VanGemeren, Willem A. "Psalms." In *The Expositor's Bible Commentary,* edited by F. Gaebelin. Grand Rapids, Mich.: Zondervan, 1991.

Walton, J. H. *Genesis.* NIV Application Commentary. Grand Rapids, Mich.: Zondervan, 2001.

Wenham, Gordon J. *Genesis 1–15* and *Genesis 16–50.* Word Biblical Commentaries. Waco, Tex.: Word, 1987 and 1994.

Wilson, Gerald H. *Psalms 1-75.* NIV Application Commentary. Grand Rapids, Mich.: Zondervan, 2003.

For Married Couples

The married couples in your group will, of course, have a history in their relationship, and that history will be as varied as the number of couples in the group. These studies should provide wonderful opportunities for couples to share relationship stories with each other. Of course, couples will be forthcoming and revealing only as they feel confidence and trust in the others.

It is likely that even persons who have been married for quite a while will not have thought intentionally about their spouse as a creature fashioned in the image of God. On the other hand, it probably won't be a hard sell to convince people that they and their spouse are sinners!

For Singles and Engaged Couples

Groups composed of or including singles and engaged couples will likely face an exactly opposite situation. Before marriage it is tempting and easy to think of marriage as the solution to problems of loneliness and sexual need. While those in a serious relationship are probably aware of their beloved's shortcomings, it is natural to gloss over them or think they are easily fixable. In this situation, it will be important to remind group members that when two sinners are joined together in marriage, problems aren't solved—they are multiplied!

FAMILY TIES

Marriages have implications beyond just a husband and a wife. What ties a family together?

Topics and Passages

Study 1: Family Traditions (Exodus 12:1-16; Matthew 26:17-30)

Study 2: Family Stories (Deuteronomy 6:20-25; Psalm 78:1-8)

Study 3: Family Traumas (2 Samuel 12:1-16; Philippians 3:12-14)

Study 4: Family Comparisons (Genesis 37:2-8)

Study 5: Family Legalism (Colossians 2:14-23)

Study 6: A Spiritual Legacy (selections from Proverbs)

Marriages have implications beyond just a husband and a wife.

Key Points

1. Family traditions include a family's celebrative remembrances of past events and other regular times to mark special occasions.
2. Since the Christian faith is based on events in history, most notably the death and resurrection of Christ, it is a tradition-based religion.
3. However, traditions can become dead when they are observed without heartfelt passion.
4. Traditions serve the value of creating family bonds.
5. Not all traditions that encourage family bonds have a specific spiritual dimension—for example, birthdays and New Year's Eve.
6. Husbands and wives need to negotiate what traditions will be important for their family.
7. A married couple must also decide together how they will interact with the traditions of their parents.
8. We reveal our faith and ourselves to our spouse by telling each other stories about our past.
9. Intimate marriages are built on a willingness to share stories.
10. Not all stories about the past are uplifting, since many people experience some form of family trauma as they grow up.
11. Sin has consequences, and sins within families often have repercussions for the generations that follow.
12. It is important for couples to be open to each other concerning the traumas of the past.
13. Family dynamics may become a source of great frustration unless observed and regulated.
14. Legalism is the creation of requirements beyond those required by God himself.
15. Legalism stifles spiritual and relational growth.
16. Marriages bequeath a spiritual legacy to their descendants, and it can be traumatic or edifying.

Synopsis

What ties a family together? This study guide begins to answer that question with a look at family traditions (study one). Christianity is a faith founded in historical events, with traditions (especially the Lord's Supper) that serve to remind us of those key events. While this example is a church-based tradition, families will establish both spiritual traditions (perhaps a daily time of reading Scripture and praying together) and traditions that are not specifically religious but serve to unite the family. Decorating the Christmas tree in a certain way and at a certain time together is one example. A new couple will have to negotiate how to relate to the traditions of the families they have just left. Will they celebrate Christmas with the husband's family or the wife's, or will they establish their own traditions? There is not a right or wrong answer to such a question, but great sensitivity will have to be exercised in areas like this that prove to be volatile.

Study two focuses on the fact that the ties between a couple and within a family become much stronger through telling and hearing stories about the past. In the first place, the Bible presents a grand narrative about the world, and we must find our place in that story. But our own lives also form a story that is worth telling, especially to our spouse. In telling our stories we reveal who we are and we learn about our spouse. Our stories are stories of faith, recounting what has happened in our past; they are expressions of our present love, and they articulate our dreams about the future.

Our stories are stories of faith, recounting what has happened in our past; they are expressions of our present love, and they articulate our dreams about the future.

Not all family stories will be positive and encouraging, so study three looks at family traumas. Painful family memories cannot be ignored, because they often have implications for the future. A strong marriage will be a safe place for wife and husband to share with each other the difficulties of the past.

Another area of potential conflict comes with children. Children can bring life's greatest joys and sharpest pain. Often spouses come with different philosophies of childrearing, and when things go wrong—and they will inevitably do so from time to time—it is easy to blame the other spouse's different approach to discipline. It is also easy to fall into subtle forms of favoritism or using a relationship with a child to compensate or vie for a better relationship with a spouse. Study four looks at such questions through the prism of the story of Joseph and his relationships to his parents and his brothers.

Study five recognizes that God does have certain behavior requirements for his people. Though we are saved by grace and not by works, we are not supposed to run wild in the streets. Yet we have a tendency to add requirements that aren't in Scripture. Legalism can paralyze our relationships with God and our spouse, so this study helps us recognize and address this harmful tendency.

The final study of the book recognizes that a marriage has future implications. Most marriages lead to childrearing, and how the spouses live out their marriage will have great significance for their children. A number of proverbs are examined to encourage couples to model godliness to the next generation.

Further Resources

These studies are from the following biblical books: Genesis, Exodus, Deuteronomy, 2 Samuel, Psalms, Matthew and Colossians. Commentaries on Genesis and Psalms are listed in the synopsis of *The Goal of Marriage*, above. The following commentaries are highly recommended for those who want to study the other books more carefully.

Arnold, B. T. *1 and 2 Samuel.* NIV Application Commentary. Grand Rapids, Mich.: Zondervan, 2003.

Enns, Peter. *Exodus.* NIV Application Commentary. Grand Rapids, Mich.: Zondervan, 2000.

Garland, D. E. *Colossians/Philemon.* NIV Application Commentary. Grand Rapids, Mich.: Zondervan, 1998.

Wilkins, Michael J. *Matthew.* NIV Application Commentary. Grand Rapids, Mich.: Zondervan, 2004.

Wright, Christopher J. H. *Deuteronomy.* New International Biblical Commentary. Peabody, Mass.: Hendrickson, 1996.

For Married Couples

Young married couples especially are in the midst of figuring out how to relate to their family of origin (parents and siblings) and to their new family (spouse and children). This study of traditions and stories as well as the dangers of trauma and legalism will help them in that process.

For Singles and Engaged Couples

Of course singles, like married couples, are in families. Everyone has to negotiate family ties at some level. This study guide will help unmarried people reflect on their family connections and also explore what marriage might be like should they decide to move in that direction.

COMMUNICATION

Wise words between a husband and a wife build a marriage up; foolish words tear it down.

Topics and Passages

Study 1: The Power of Words (Genesis 1:1-8; selections from Proverbs)

Study 2: Talk That Hurts Relationships (selections from Proverbs)

Study 3: Talk That Builds Relationships (selections from Proverbs)

Study 4: A Time to Be Quiet and a Time to Speak Up (Ecclesiastes 3:1-7; selections from Proverbs)

Study 5: The Art of Listening and Reflection (selections from Proverbs)

Study 6: The Couple That Prays Together . . . (1 Corinthians 7:3-6; Romans 8:22-23, 26-27)

Key Points

1. Words are powerful. They can create and build up or destroy relationships.
2. Words are means of disclosing oneself and learning about others.
3. Conversation is a divinely appointed tool for weaving two lives together.
4. Contemptuous speech is particularly corrosive to a marriage relationship.
5. *When* something is said is as important as *what* is said.
6. The book of Proverbs is a particularly helpful resource to learn how to speak wisely and avoid foolish speech.
7. Wise speech builds the other person up.
8. While wise speech is always spoken with kind intentions, it may include constructive criticism that the hearer will find hard to receive.
9. Men typically speak less than women. To avoid unproductive conflict, each spouse needs to be sensitive to the speech patterns of the other.
10. It is important to develop listening skills.
11. Good listening is more than hearing; it is also acting on what is heard.
12. A couple that prays together enhances their marriage by keeping its foundation secure.

Conversation is a divinely appointed tool for weaving two lives together.

Synopsis

- Sticks and stone may break my bones . . .
- It's just talk.
- Talk is cheap.

These common expressions suggest that there is nothing to words. While when voiced at the right time these statements can be true, it is absolutely false that words mean nothing. Words are the tools of connection between human beings. They are means of self-disclosure and revelation between two people. We share ourselves and we learn about others through conversation. Nothing could be more important to a relationship of any kind than high-quality words. Words are especially critical to the process of weaving two lives into a strong marriage.

The first study looks at biblical texts that suggest the power of words. This power can be seen particularly in divine words. When God speaks, he creates and destroys by the power of his words. Human beings do not have the same measure of power, of course, but our being created in God's image means that our words do carry significance. They can build up or tear down relationships.

Study two looks more closely at what the book of Proverbs calls foolish speech. Foolish speech tears down relational bonds. Contemptuous speech is particularly damaging. For all speech, timing is important. It is vitally important to be sensitive to how your spouse will hear what you are saying.

Study three examines the other side of Proverbs' teaching on speech: what constitutes wise speech. Wise speech is often kind, gentle and encouraging. However, wise speech may also contain criticism. After all, it is not kind to let someone keep repeating a mistaken behavior that will land them in trouble or hurt others. Wise persons avoid pride in their speech, and they don't allow pride to block their ability to hear criticism.

The next study (four) explores the issue of the timing of speech more fully. It also addresses the fact that women typically enjoy conversation more than men. This is not a stereotype; the different hardwiring of the genders in relation to speech has been demonstrated through empirical studies. Negotiating this difference is an important issue in marriage relationships. In this study the tendency to form demilitarized zones (DMZ) is recognized. These are areas where couples avoid conversation because they know it will inevitably lead to conflict.

While the first four studies focus on speaking, study five reflects on the importance of listening. In particular, it explores the wisdom of listening to criticism and not letting pride get in the way.

Finally, study six reminds us that a strong marriage has a strong foundation in a relationship with God. Thus husbands and wives should talk to God "without ceasing," both individually and corporately.

Further Resources

These studies are from the following biblical books: Genesis, Proverbs, Ecclesiastes, Romans, 1 Corinthians, Ephesians, Philippians, Matthew, Colossians and 1 Thessalonians. Commentaries on Genesis, Psalms, Ecclesiastes, Matthew and Colossians are listed in the previous synopses. The following commentaries on the other books are highly recommended for those who want to study these passages more carefully.

Blomberg, Craig. *1 Corinthians.* NIV Application Commentary. Grand Rapids, Mich.: Zondervan, 1994.

Holmes, M. W. *1 and 2 Thessalonians.* NIV Application Commentary. Grand Rapids, Mich.: Zondervan, 1998.

Koptak, P. *Proverbs.* NIV Application Commentary. Grand Rapids, Mich.: Zondervan, 2003.

Longman, Tremper, III. *Proverbs.* Grand Rapids, Mich.: Baker, 2006.

Moo, Douglas J. *Romans.* NIV Application Commentary. Grand Rapids, Mich.: Zondervan, 2000.

Snodgrass, K. *Ephesians.* NIV Application Commentary. Grand Rapids, Mich.: Zondervan, 1996.

Thielman, Frank. *Philippians.* NIV Application Commentary. Grand Rapids, Mich.: Zondervan, 1995.

For Married Couples

These studies will allow married couples to examine their communication patterns and consider how they might be enriched. After being married awhile most husbands and wives have fallen into some kind of routine, skirting topics that are too volatile to handle (DMZs). However, avoiding talking about difficult issues is not healthy. Principles of good conversation derived from Proverbs and elsewhere are applied to marriage.

For Singles and Engaged Couples

In the first place, it is good to establish healthy lines of communication before marriage. Furthermore, principles of good speaking and listening are applicable to all types of human relationships.

MALE & FEMALE

Men and women are both created equally in the image of God but are also wonderfully different.

Topics and Passages

Study 1: Gender Differences (Genesis 3:16-19)

Study 2: Who's in Charge? (Galatians 3:26—4:7)

Study 3: The Ten-Letter Dirty Word: S-U-B-M-I-S-S-I-O-N (Ephesians 5:21-33; Philippians 2:3-4)

Study 4: The Godly Wife (Proverbs 31:10-31)

Study 5: The Godly Husband (Psalm 112)

Study 6: Reflecting the Glory of God Together (Joshua 5:13-15; Psalm 131)

Key Points

1. Men and women are equal before God but different from each other.
2. Women tend to find their significance more in relationship and men in work.
3. This does not mean that women do not work and find joy in it any more than it means that men don't find satisfaction in relationships. It is a difference of degree, not of kind.
4. Women and men were created equal in the presence of God.
5. Husbands and wives are to live in a relationship of mutual submission.
6. To submit to another is not to simply do what the other says nor to be the other's slave.
7. Submission is putting the other person ahead of one's own agenda.
8. The core of being a godly wife or a godly husband is "the fear of the LORD."
9. Both males and females, husbands and wives, reflect the glory of God.

> *Submission is putting the other person ahead of one's own agenda.*

Synopsis

The issue of the differences between men and women is fraught with potential dangers. It is important to recognize from the start that the Bible does not establish specific roles for the different genders. But there are differences between men and women beyond the obvious anatomical ones. Study one approaches that question by looking at God's punishment of Adam and Eve after the Fall. It is illuminating to see that God punishes Adam in the realm of work and Eve in the realm of relationship. It is not that men are not interested in relationship or that women are not interested in work. But differences in each gender's focus are acknowledged in every culture; in our own, a book like John Gray's

Men Are from Mars, Women Are from Venus (1992) achieved great popularity because it hit a nerve. The secular social psychologist Carol Gilligan has highlighted gender differences in her *In a Different Voice: Psychological Theory and Women's Development* (1993).

Studies two and three take up potentially controversial areas. Christians strongly disagree on a number of these issues, and the study of Galatians 3 and Ephesians 5 will bring these out. These passages, however, are best summarized as teaching that men and women are equal and that in marriage a husband and wife are to put their spouse's agenda above their own. Precisely what it means to put one's spouse's agenda ahead of one's own is not always clear, and these studies will lead to discussions that will help couples negotiate what mutual submission should look like in their relationship.

The next two studies (four and five) take a look at two passages (Proverbs 31:10-31 and Psalm 112) that describe what it means to be a godly woman and a godly man. Many of the characteristics are the same, especially the shaping of their fundamental character by "the fear of the LORD."

Finally, we study texts (study six) that show that both females and males reflect the glory of God. After all, both are created in the image of God. This explains why Scripture uses both male (king, warrior, etc.) and female (mother, woman teacher, etc.) images for God. Neither male nor female is closer to God.

The fact that women and men are created in the image of God also means that we can learn about God by studying how God's nature is reflected in our spouse.

Further Resources

These studies are from the following books: Genesis, Joshua, Psalms, Proverbs, Galatians, Ephesians and Philippians. Commentaries on all but Joshua and Galatians are listed in the previous synopses. The following commentaries are highly recommended for those who want to study those books more carefully.

Howard, David M. *Joshua.* New American Commentary. Nashville: Broadman & Holman, 1998.

McKnight, Scot. *Galatians.* NIV Application Commentary. Grand Rapids, Mich.: Zondervan, 1995.

For Married Couples

Married couples need to come to grips with male and female equality as well as differences. Understanding both will help wives and husbands appreciate and understand each other better. The fact that women and men are created in the image of God also means that we can learn about God by studying how God's nature is reflected in our spouse.

For Singles and Engaged Couples

One doesn't have to be married to recognize that there are differences between men and women. Indeed, working through this study not only will prepare singles and engaged couples for marriage but also will help men understand their female friends and associates better and vice versa.

FORGIVENESS

Marriage unites two sinners in an intimate relationship and thus becomes a crucible for repentance and forgiveness that leads to reconciliation and enhanced love.

Topics and Passages

Study 1: What God has Brought Together . . . (Genesis 3:1-7)

Study 2: Sin Separates (Romans 7:7-25)

Study 3: Coming to Grips with One's Failures (Psalm 51)

Study 4: No Cheap Grace (Luke 17:1-4)

Study 5: The Log and the Speck (Matthew 7:1-6; 18:21-35)

Study 6: The Joys of Forgiveness (Luke 15:11-32)

Key Points

1. Sin rips apart relationships.
2. Marriage brings together two sinners in an intimate relationship.
3. The first step toward reconciliation is recognition that my sin has harmed the one I love.
4. Since marriage brings together two sinners, it is a crucible for repentance and forgiveness.
5. Love will lead a husband or wife to help their spouse come to recognize their failures.
6. Criticism must be done with humility and not with a sense of self-righteousness.
7. Forgiveness must be freely offered to those who repent.
8. Repentance must prove to be genuine if forgiveness is to move to reconciliation.
9. Conflict left alone moves people apart.
10. Conflict that leads through repentance and forgiveness to reconciliation enhances mutual love.

Synopsis

All healthy marriages go through conflict. Only superficial relationships escape it. What is important for spouses is not avoiding all conflict but knowing how to negotiate differences when they arise. This study guide offers a biblical strategy for dealing with conflict: recognizing sin, asking for and receiving forgiveness, and reconciling.

Study one looks at the origin of sin in the rebellion of Adam and Eve. Here we learn that self-centeredness is at the heart of sin. It is considering oneself the most important thing in the universe. Of course, such pride is poisonous to relationship. In a strong relationship, each treats the other with respect and deference.

Study two continues to look at sin and the way it divides people, including spouses. Romans 7 shows that sin not only alienates people from each other but also tears people up inside.

Study three looks at Psalm 51, composed by David after his sin with Bathsheba was exposed. His first step is recognizing his failure and turning toward God and away from his sin. Often such self-awareness of one's sin comes through the criticism of another.

Study four highlights the reality that grace is not cheap. Though a person should be ready to offer forgiveness, it is not done automatically. Forgiveness follows sincere repentance.

Our fifth study looks at Jesus' teaching about "the log and the speck" and points out how important it is for an offended spouse to approach the other with a measure of humility and without self-righteousness. This makes it easier for the other to hear and respond to criticism without defensiveness.

> ### *Self-centeredness is at the heart of sin.*

The final study takes a look at the parable of the prodigal son. Here we see reconciliation at work, leading to joy. When we have been forgiven, we gain a greater appreciation and love for the one who has offered forgiveness.

Further Resources

These studies are from the following books: Genesis, Psalms, Matthew, Luke and Romans. Commentaries on all but Luke are listed in the previous synopses. The following commentary on Luke is highly recommended for those who want to study that book more carefully.

Bock, Darrell L. *Luke.* NIV Application Commentary. Grand Rapids, Mich.: Zondervan, 1996.

For Married Couples

You don't have to be married long before you realize that close relationships have their struggles. As sinners, husbands and wives will often seek what is best for them rather than for their spouse. The only relationships that escape conflict are those that remain superficial. This study allows married couples to consider whether they are handling their struggles in a biblical manner. The study will point out that marriage is a crucible for repentance and forgiveness. This is good news, though, since one who has been forgiven much loves much.

For Singles and Engaged Couples

Many unmarried people have an idealized view of marriage. They are lonely and think that marriage will once and for all solve their loneliness. At the same time, other singles fear marriage because of the struggles they have seen in their parents' relationship. In any case, it is vitally important that singles and engaged couples are aware that marriage brings together two sinners in an intimate relationship. They need to prepare ahead of time for handling conflicts in a godly way.

SEXUAL INTIMACY

In spite of obstacles, a husband and wife are encouraged to explore and enjoy each other's body in an act of giving and receiving pleasure.

Topics and Passages

Study 1: Desire and Ecstasy (Song of Songs 6:13—7:13)

Study 2: Different Bodies (Song of Songs 4:1—5:1, 10-16)

Study 3: Time for Passion (Song of Songs 1:2-4, 7-17)

Study 4: Overcoming Contempt and Shame (Genesis 2:25—3:17; 2 Samuel 6:14-16, 20-22)

Study 5: Restoring Broken Trust (Psalm 55)

Study 6: Love's Failure and Redemption (Song of Songs 5:1—6:3)

Key Points

1. Sex is God's good gift to his creatures.
2. The Song of Songs is a major resource to help Christians understand God's attitude toward our sexual enjoyment.
3. Sex is reserved for marriage alone and should be enjoyed to its fullest in that context.
4. Sensuous pleasure involves more than an orgasm; it begins with foreplay.
5. The evil one hates sex and will do everything he can to undermine the physical pleasure of a wife and a husband.

6. Chief among the tools employed by evil to destroy sexual enjoyment are the relationship-dividing emotions of contempt, shame and fear.

7. While the Bible certainly affirms that one's relationship with God is more important than beauty (Proverbs 31:30), the Song of Songs reminds us that it is appropriate to desire beauty and enhance our attractiveness for the benefit of our spouse.

8. The Song of Songs models how a couple speaks lovingly to each other in a way that encourages them toward sexual union.

9. Beauty involves more than physical attributes. It involves a person's character and personality.

Synopsis

God directed Adam to leave his parents and weave a new life with his wife, and then they would cleave in sexual intimacy (Genesis 2:24). This study guide explores the culminating act of sexual intimacy.

The presence of the Song of Songs in the canon is the surest indication that God loves for his creatures to enjoy sex in marriage. Sex is a wonderfully powerful gift, but it is also potentially dangerous. People can experience the greatest joy and the most severe pain in this area of their life. Because of the dangers and the importance of preserving this joy, God set boundaries restricting the sexual act to a married man and woman (Exodus 20:14; 1 Corinthians 6:12-20). But within those boundaries, the Song of Songs reminds us that a husband and wife are free to play with and enjoy each other.

For this reason, most of the studies in this guide are based on the Song of Songs. Many Christians know very little about this biblical book. It seems odd that such a sensuous book is in the canon. Indeed, some interpreters have tried to desex it by turning it into an allegory of the relationship between Jesus and the church. While it is true that Scripture compares our relationship with Jesus to a marriage (Ephesians 5:21-33), the Song is a book about human relationships.

God loves for his creatures to enjoy sex in marriage.

The Song is composed of love poems. It tells no story; the poems are to be taken as they appear, poetic expressions of a woman and a man in love and desiring physical union with one another. One of the hardest aspects of interpreting the Song is unpacking the many metaphors and similes each uses to describe the spouse's body and feelings toward each other. The study guide contains resources to help you unpack the images.

The first study explores desire and ecstasy. Sometimes Christians struggle with sexual desire even within the context of marriage. This struggle is especially strong in women and men whose parents have told them or given them the impression for years that sex is dirty. Or perhaps they are just repelled by the way society has turned sex into an idol. Another source of struggles may be a history of promiscuity that has led to guilt. However, a study of the Song encourages Christians to embrace their feelings of desire and longing for ecstasy within marriage.

Study two explores the issue of physical beauty. While some biblical passages teach that beauty is not very important, the Song dwells on exquisite descriptions of the male and female bodies. How can couples help each other overcome their feelings of physical inadequacy?

When many think of sex, they focus on the orgasm, a moment of ecstasy that, though wonderful, is short. However, study three points out that sex means more than orgasm. It is a process that involves a long buildup. The best sex begins with foreplay.

Even the Song of Songs, however, understands that sex faces obstacles to enjoyment. God loves sex and has given it as a good gift to his creatures. No wonder the evil one works hard at undermining and perverting such a great source of enjoyment. Studies four and five combine to look at three major roadblocks to sexual intimacy: contempt, fear and shame. Intimate relationships are destroyed when either partner, overwhelmed by any of these emotions, attacks or flees from the other.

So as our final study will indicate, at times a person moves toward their spouse seeking intimacy but instead finds coldness or hostility. After all, wives and husbands are still sinners, and sin results in rupture in relationships. However, the dramatic poem of Song of Songs 5:1—6:3 describes ultimate union after initial alienation.

Further Resources

These studies are from four biblical books: Genesis, 2 Samuel, Psalms and Song of Songs. Commentaries on Genesis, 2 Samuel and Psalms are listed in previous synopses. The following commentary on Song of Songs is highly recommended for those who want to study these passages more carefully.

Longman, Tremper, III. *Song of Songs*. New International Commentary. Grand Rapids, Mich.: Eerdmans, 2001.

See also the commentary by Iain Provan on both Ecclesiastes and Song of Songs listed in the *Goal of Marriage* summary.

For Married Couples

This study guide is geared toward married couples who presently are in a relationship that allows them to enjoy God's good gift of sex. However, the leaders should go in with eyes wide open to the fact that most married couples struggle in their sexual life. Different histories, levels of desire and expectations may mean that anger and disappointment are dominating a relationship rather than joy. In this study, it may be a good idea to give people more space to think and talk alone and especially with their spouse, since some questions and insights may be too personal for them to articulate openly in a group.

For Singles and Engaged Couples

The Bible is clear: sex is reserved for marriage. However, that does not mean that singles and especially engaged couples can't talk about it. Singles will want to know just how far they can go before they cross a boundary. What is appropriate physically between two unmarried people? The Bible is clear that intercourse is reserved for marriage, but what about kissing, hugging, petting? There is no direct biblical teaching about this, so the leaders will do well to think ahead of time about this question. Certain behaviors are so close to intercourse that they seem obviously off limits. But it would seem draconian to suggest that *all* physical contact is off limits before marriage. One principle that may be kept in mind for discussion is whether the level of physical intimacy goes up the more serious, exclusive and committed a relationship becomes.

A word to the wise: the Song of Songs, as part of the Bible, contains God's wisdom for everyone, so singles should not be excluded. But sometimes the Song stirs up desires that can't be satisfied, and this can lead to frustration and anger.

DREAMS & DEMANDS

Strong marriages recognize and have a plan to handle anticipated points of conflict: children, money, jealousy, boredom and past abuse. A wise couple will also avail themselves of the support and advice of their fellow believers in these areas.

Topics and Passages

Study 1: Fruitful or Barren? (Genesis 30:1-8)

Study 2: For Richer or for Poorer (Proverbs 30:5-9; Matthew 6:19-34)

Study 3: Jealousy: The Passion to Protect—or Destroy (Song of Songs 8:6-8; 1 Corinthians 13:4-6)

Study 4: Feeling No Connection (Ecclesiastes 1:8-10; 9:7-10)

Study 5: Wounded Heart (2 Samuel 13:1-22)

Study 6: It Takes a Church . . . (selections from Proverbs)

Key Points

1. The birth of children, while a blessing, sometimes leads a couple to neglecting their marriage relationship.
2. A husband and wife must be intentional in maintaining the vitality of their relationship as they raise children.
3. Money—how to make it and how to spend it—can be a point of conflict between a husband and a wife.
4. Jealousy can be a good thing if it represents energy to preserve a marriage that is being threatened by a rival.
5. Jealousy can be destructive if suspicions are ill-founded or if, under any circumstances, it is expressed in a violent way.
6. Boredom leads to disengagement, which can harm and even destroy a marriage.
7. Boredom occurs when life becomes overly predictable.
8. A couple should be intentional about thinking and planning together to engender passion and surprise in their relationship.
9. A traumatic past can resurface to harm a present relationship.
10. To maintain a strong marriage, spouses need to avail themselves of the support and advice of their fellow believers.

> *Jealousy can be a good thing if it represents energy to preserve a marriage that is being threatened by a rival.*

Synopsis

The marriage of two sinners does not solve the problem of sin; if anything, it intensifies it. The unique nature of marriage means that there are certain realms where one can expect particularly strong tensions to arise.

Children are a blessing from the Lord, and most parents anticipate the presence of daughters and sons with great excitement. But it is true that people have only so much energy and time, and children require abundant doses of each. Some couples make the fatal mistake of putting their marriage on hold as they raise their children. Study one reflects on dangers and remedies.

Money (study two) represents one's values. How one works to make money and where one chooses to spend it reveals a lot about a person. A wife and husband may have different ideas about money, and this can lead to tension. Assorted Scripture passages are studied in order to induce conversation about this area of potential conflict.

In the third study participants will reflect on marriage's unique character as the only mutually exclusive relationship. A person can have one and only one spouse. Rivals are not to be tolerated. But what happens when there is a threat to a marriage? Is jealousy ever a proper emotion?

From the white-hot passion of jealousy, study four goes on to consider the dangers that boredom brings to a relationship. After early intensity, some relationships subside into bland routine. Participants will reflect on the dangers of boredom and suggest some ways out.

Another source of potential trouble for a marriage comes from the past. A traumatic upbringing, particularly physical and sexual abuse, can resurface, creating issues for a married couple.

Finally, study six reminds us that though there are many things that work to unravel a marriage, God has provided support in the form of the church.

Further Resources

These studies are from the following biblical books: Genesis, 2 Samuel, Proverbs, Ecclesiastes, Song of Songs, Matthew and 1 Corinthians. Commentaries on all of these are listed in the previous synopses.

For Married Couples

These studies will help married couples identify points of conflict within their relationship. It will further give them the opportunity to develop strategies for confronting these issues and not relegating them to a DMZ. It will also remind them that they do not have to depend on themselves but can benefit from relationships in the broader Christian community.

For Singles and Engaged Couples

An ounce of prevention . . . Singles and especially engaged couples will be better equipped to deal with later conflicts if they begin to negotiate these potentially incendiary topics in anticipation of marriage. Also, a number of these points of tension, like money, are issues with which everyone has to struggle.

A MARRIAGE SERMON SERIES

This chapter presents four sermons on marriage. These are actual sermons, so the anecdotes are personal. The intention, of course, is not that these sermons be delivered "as is" but that they stimulate thinking as preachers contextualize the passages to their own congregation and in reference to their own life situation.

SERMON ONE: GOD'S STRATEGY FOR A "SUCCESSFUL" MARRIAGE

Genesis 2:18-25

I am preaching this morning on God's plan for marriage from Genesis 2. Now I need to make a couple of preliminary comments. First, I am preaching on a subject that is not immediately relevant to all of you. In other words, not all of you are married. Some of you are single: some are so by choice, and some of you would prefer to be married. Some of you have been through the pain of divorce. Some of you have even lost a spouse to death.

Even if you aren't married, though, you can learn from today's passage. You can learn about God and his wisdom. If you are single, you one day may be married, so it is good to think about these things in advance. You don't know what God has in store for you. And as we will see at the end of the sermon, through a better understanding of the biblical idea of marriage we can all come to a deeper understanding of our relationship with Jesus Christ.

Furthermore, by studying marriage we can learn significant principles about relationships in general. Marriage is the most intense and intimate of all human relationships, and so aspects of it, especially the sexual parts, are not relevant to friendships. But a number of the principles *are* helpful to understanding how other relationship work.

Even though there is a danger that some of you will feel left out by the topic, it is still important to address the issue of marriage from the pulpit because it is such a source of joy and pain in our lives. Divorce statistics are staggering. Last I heard the rate was around 50 percent, and even higher among younger couples. It is also discouraging to hear that some studies have indicated that Christian marriages fare no better than non-Christian marriages. Of course statistics lie; Gary Oliver, a Christian psychologist, is doing a more careful study of the latter, since he believes that you have to do more than just ask someone if they are a Christian to count them in that category.

But even if it turns out to be true that there are fewer divorces than the statistics are presently suggesting, we must grapple with the fact that many Christian marriages struggle. As we will see, God established the institution of marriage to deal with the problem of human loneliness. If that is so, why are so many married people lonely? When I speak to unmarried college kids, I find they think it is the solution to all their problems, both their loneliness and their sexual desires. Those who have been married for a while know that they still get lonely, though, and they still struggle with sexual issues.

Through a better understanding of the biblical idea of marriage we can all come to a deeper understanding of our relationship with Jesus Christ.

Thus it is important to see God's wisdom in regard to marriage, and what better place to go than to the beginning when God created marriage? We will first look at what leads up to the first marriage and note the significance of how God created woman. Then we will focus on God's requirements for a marriage. As we will see, they are that the man and the woman leave their past life, weave a life together and then cleave together in an intimate embrace.

So let me begin by reading through Genesis 2:18-23, the verses that lead up to God's "leave, weave and cleave" command.

If you think about it, it is pretty amazing that the man was lonely. After all, God created a world with abundant resources for him. But even more significant than his garden surroundings, *God* had an intimate relationship with Adam. Adam was created from the dust of the ground, showing his relationship to his fellow creatures, but only he was an-imated by the very breath of God. The previous chapter of Genesis also tells us that he was created in the image of God, which means that he reflects who God is. Even with this special relationship with God, Adam was lonely. God does not condemn him for this but rather works to remedy his loneliness.

God is going to make a "helper" for Adam. Now I need to pause here and comment on this word *helper*. It almost gives you the idea that God plans on creating a servant for Adam. And indeed some people have read this verse with the idea that the woman is the man's inferior. But if you look at how this word is used elsewhere in the Old Testament, you will notice that God himself is called the helper of Israel (Exodus 18:4; Psalm 70:5). Certainly these passages do not suggest that God is a subordinate servant to Israel. So there is no subordination of the woman implied in the word *helper*.

As God gets started locating the helper who will dispel Adam's loneliness, we kind of scratch our head. He starts parading the animals in front of him. Adam names them, but he doesn't find a helper suitable for him. Well, of course not. They are animals! Did God really think Adam would find his partner this way?

Did God really think Adam would find his partner [by viewing a parade of all the animals]? No. God is just building up the excitement, . . . paving the way for Adam's recognition of his proper partner.

No. God is just building up the excitement. By showing what will not work, God is paving the way for Adam's recognition of his proper partner.

God then creates Eve from Adam's rib. What is the significance? Side. Equals, partners. Not from the head and not from the foot. As Matthew Henry said in the nineteenth century: "Not made out of his head to top him, not out of his feet to be trampled upon by him, but out of his side to be equal with him, under his arm to be protected, and near his heart to be beloved."

We now come to the divine pronouncement that gets to the heart of marriage: "This explains why a man leaves his father and mother and is joined to his wife, and the two are united into one."

This is what I am calling leaving, weaving and cleaving. What is a marriage? A marriage is a relationship between a man and a woman in which they have left their parents, they have woven a life together and they cleave together in an intimate embrace. Let's look at these three parts and try to understand them better.

Leaving

Why is it important that a woman and a man leave their mother and father in order to have a happy marriage? And what does it mean to leave anyway?

Well, leaving one's parents does not necessarily mean physically leaving them. After all, in the ancient Near East—and we see this in the stories of Genesis that follow—it was typical for a new married couple to actually live in the household of their parents. It is very unlikely that this passage should be understood to command a kind of physical abandonment of parents.

Our friends can't be more important to us than our wife. Women, your girlfriends can't be more important to you than your husband.

It also does not mean that a married couple avoids seeking advice or refuses to accept financial help from their parents.

What does it mean then? It means that a married couple must establish a new primary loyalty. In the past, the man and woman had their parents as their primary family relationship. If she needed advice, a young woman would go to her parents. If he needed guidance or help, a man would go to his parents. After marriage, though, the new primary loyalty is to one's spouse.

I should also point out that though the text talks about leaving parents, there are other things from the past that a new married couple will have to leave if they are to establish a healthy relationship. Perhaps friends or habits will have to be left—again, not necessarily literally and absolutely, but in terms of primary loyalty. Our friends can't be more important to us than our wife. Women, your girlfriends can't be more important to you than your husband. If you want a healthy marriage, your relationship with your spouse has to be your most important human relationship.

Thus it is important to build boundaries around the new relationship that will allow trust and confidence to grow. These boundaries will have to be worked out by the couple together. It is absolutely critical that a wife and husband foster a relationship in which they can point out to each other where they feel that boundary is being transgressed.

And not only newlyweds need to hear this. Couples married a long time do as well.

For more years than I want to admit, I had the annoying habit of reverting to my youth whenever Alice and I would visit my parents. I would act like a kid again when we visited them. When Alice would point this out, I kind of thought it was funny, but in retrospect I see it as a failure to leave home.

As for me, I felt that Alice had failed to leave home when it came to fixing things around the house. Her stepfather was Mr. Fixit. I couldn't tell a hammer from a screwdriver. Just mentioning that something needed fixing around our place was enough to send me into a cold sweat. I figured you could pay to get something fixed. And when I failed to fix something she might say something like "Well, I guess I am just used to having a man around the house that knew what he was doing."

Though I say this, I also recognize that in other areas we did leave our parents and establish a new primary loyalty. And the fact that we depended on each other and not on our parents gave us room to grow in our relationship.

Weaving

But a new husband and wife do not leave their parents just to leave. It is with the intention of weaving a new relationship.

By the way, it is in this area that we can learn the most about friendships. Only marriage requires a leaving to start. After all, marriage is the only mutually exclusive relationship. You can have many friends but only one spouse. And as we will see in relation to cleaving, God's will is that sexual intimacy be reserved for marriage. But while weaving a marriage relationship may involve a particularly intense kind of intimacy, friends also can bond closely.

Weaving two lives together is a process. It does not happen overnight, and in one sense it is never perfect or complete. No matter how compatible a husband and wife are, weaving requires doing things together and talking together.

And that's hard, especially for twenty-first-century Americans. We lead hectic lives. We are torn by work, children, myriad commitments. We find it hard to do things together and to talk together. Wives and husbands are often flying by each other, each on their way to a separate event.

But there are more problems than simply the modern cultural moment. It appears that men and women are hardwired differently. There have been studies of how men and women speak. This is generalizing—it is not true of every woman and every man—but on average a woman speaks something like 20,000 words a day and a man about 5,000. The problem is compounded in families where there are young children and the mother stays home with the children all day. Imagine the husband going off to work and speaking 14,500 words in the context of his work all day. His wife is home, and she has spoken 5,000 words, and 4,900 of them are *no*. The husband comes home; he has 500 words left. The woman has 35,000 words left. This is a formula for disaster.

Alice and I have been married for thirty-two years. Like all couples, we have gone through seasons of life. I have to confess that it is easy for me to stand up here and tell you all to make time to talk. It would be easy to tell you that our relationship has grown stronger over the past three years because we begin each day with a three-mile walk in which we talk and pray together. But I need to tell you as well that it was nearly impossible for us to do that with three young children and new careers and a hundred other things in life. Still, as I look back, I wish I had set aside even ten minutes at the beginning of each day to talk. And I encourage even those of you who are in the midst of the busyness of life to do that.

On average a woman speaks something like 20,000 words a day and a man about 5,000.

Again, the same can be said of developing friendships. You need to invest time in people in order to have friends. You need to do things with them and talk with them, share your life and be interested in theirs. For many of us, making friends is not something that happens naturally. We need to be intentional in developing friends.

What do we talk about to weave our lives together? Many things, trivial and monumental. But I want to highlight two categories: stories and dreams. As we look to the past, we tell each other stories. I don't mean made-up stories; we share our lives with each other. We need to know about the joys and pain of each other's past so we understand what makes us tick. Even in marriage this takes courage and requires an increasing level of trust of each other.

Dreams are an expression of hope for the future. What do you as an individual, as a couple, want to do today, this week, the rest of your life? Dreams shape your future, and couples need to dream together by disclosing and discussing their future aspirations.

As we speak to each other, we need to be sensitive to our differences as well. If I had my way, I would probably spend all my time talking about NFL football and what I accomplished at work. Alice might more naturally want to explore relationships. We need to develop an interest in each other's worlds as we talk.

Is all talk going to be positive and uplifting? If you have an argument, does that mean you have a bad relationship? Not at all. As a matter of fact, I would suggest that if you never, or only once in a blue moon, have had an argument, then you have a troubled relationship.

Why would I say this? Remember who we are. Yes, we are two creatures created in the image of God. But as we soon find out in Genesis 3, we are also sinful rebels. Many people enter marriage thinking that it will resolve all their problems. They forget that marriage unites two sinners. If two sinners come together, do you think it removes trouble? Of course not; it can *intensify* trouble.

We need to risk

conflict in order to

engage with the reality

of our lives.

❦

Thus if there are absolutely no conflicts between two spouses, or any two people for that matter, it is most likely because they have stayed on the surface. They have refused to enter into what my psychologist friend Dan Allender has called DMZs. Every marriage has them: subjects—perhaps money, in-laws, children or sex—that you know are going to cause friction. With Alice and me, it was how to raise the children. Our tendency is to avoid these DMZs and avoid conflict, but to do so is damaging. We need to risk conflict in order to engage with the reality of our lives.

Cleaving

The consummation of the threefold process of marriage is coming together as one flesh. Notice that the bliss of Eden is summed up in verse 25 with the statement that Eve and Adam were naked and feeling no shame.

Notice too that cleaving follows leaving and weaving. Not that each step must be carried out perfectly before you can move on to the next; as I have already said, it never happens perfectly. But better sex happens after good conversation.

Sex is a topic that is wondrous, mysterious and difficult. I will not do it full justice here. Many people think that the Bible and Christianity are down on sex. If something is too much fun, it has to be bad. And indeed, the Bible is negative in the extreme about sex outside of marriage. But the Bible is *not* negative about sex in marriage; it celebrates sexuality, and indeed there is a whole book, the Song of Songs, that talks about the passion of love in almost scandalous terms. If you don't know what I am referring to and have never read this book, do so this afternoon.

Another common misconception about the Bible and sex is that its sole or primary purpose is to generate children. Nothing could be further from the truth. Neither this passage in Genesis nor the whole of the Song of Songs mentions anything about children. The Bible celebrates marital sex in terms of its sensual pleasure, the joy of giving to and receiving physical pleasure from each other. God tells us to leave, weave and cleave, not leave, weave, cleave and heave (in childbirth).

But the sad and difficult truth is that sex often brings as much pain as it does pleasure. Fear, distrust and shame enter in and rob us of joy in this area. In Genesis 2 we see Adam and Eve standing naked before each other and feeling no shame. That changes in the very next chapter because of Eve and Adam's sin. They cover themselves up. They can no longer stand in front of each other without shame.

Another aspect of the message of the Song of Songs, though, is that redemption is possible for our marital relationship, because in this book we see a man and woman naked, in a garden again, and enjoying one another's body.

So as we reflect on marriage in the light of Genesis 2 we learn a lot about ourselves. Most important, we learn of the importance of leaving, weaving and cleaving to establish a solid, godly marriage together.

However, at the beginning of the talk I suggested that we would learn more from Genesis 2 than merely about our marriages. We also gain insight into our relationship with God.

In the Bible our relationship with God is compared to human relationships that people experience daily. God is our father, God is a king, God is a mother, God is a teacher, God is a warrior, God is a shepherd. And very often God is a husband.

> **Marriage is a special image of our relationship with God.**
>
> 🖝

Each one of these images throws an important and different light on the nature of God and the quality of our relationship with him. Marriage is a special image of our relationship with God because of its unique character. Only marriage is mutually exclusive, and marriage is the most intimate of all human relationships. It is important to reflect on our relationship with God in light of its being a marriage. It calls on us to love him with passion and intimacy. It reminds us that we need to be faithful and not seek after other gods.

And of course for the Christian, this theme is most pointedly expressed by Paul's words in Ephesians 5:21-33.

Much could be discussed in this passage, but I end by pointing especially to verses 31-33, which actually quote our passage from Genesis. This reminds us that there is an even greater loyalty than the one we have to our spouse, and that is to Jesus. It is on the basis of this relationship that strong marriages are built.

And next week I will speak to this point, as we look at the book of Proverbs, specifically Proverbs 9:1-6, to see that in order to have a strong marriage we must cultivate a strong relationship with God.

SERMON TWO: THE KEY TO A STRONG MARRIAGE—LOVE WOMAN WISDOM! PROVERBS 9:1-6, 13-18

You can find a lot of advice to improve your marriage out there. There are books and seminars that offer valuable advice for husbands and wives. However, my guess is that you have never heard the following advice based on the book of Proverbs anywhere else: *To love your spouse well, you must love another woman even more passionately.* Indeed, not only husbands but also wives need to love this other woman so much that their spouse is a distant second.

As a matter of fact, everyone, married or single, needs to make this woman number one in their life. So even though this sermon is specifically geared for married people, you single people need to pay attention, because having a relationship with this woman is the most important decision you will make in your life.

So we turn now to the book of Proverbs, but before we read the text which is the focus of this talk, let me say a few things about the book.

Giving the Context

Proverbs is a book that has a lot to say about many practical topics. That is probably how you know it, by its pithy advice about how to live life well. These proverbs have much to say about family life in general and marriage in particular. The book, according to its preface (1:1-7), has as its purpose the desire to make people wise. It wants to transform naive people into mature people and to make the mature even wiser.

As we get into the book, we need to recognize that it is primarily the instruction of a son by his father. This is typical of ancient Near Eastern wisdom texts, whether from Israel, Egypt or Mesopotamia, but what is interesting and unique about Proverbs is that the father says he is also representing his wife. It is the father speaking to his son, but his teaching comes from both parents (Proverbs 1:8).

Now the fact that the son is the one who is addressed in the book means that the teaching is geared toward males. As we will see, it will be important to keep in mind that the shape of the teaching is directed toward young males. Some of us who are a bit older, and especially females, may have to work harder to apply the teaching of the book, but it's worth it. We have to put ourselves in the place of the young man. We have to imagine that we are the son being addressed by the father.

I should point out that we do this whenever we read any portion of Scripture. None of the Scripture was written for a broad audience; it was always addressed to some contemporary group. Take the book of Galatians, for instance. It is written, as the name implies, to the church at Galatia. It interacts with problems in that church that we can understand only by implication. Nonetheless, by virtue of the book's presence in the canon, we understand that these words to the Galatians also contain God's word to us.

Love Woman Wisdom, Spurn Woman Folly

As I said, the book of Proverbs teaches a lot directly about marriage and also has much practical advice for how people should speak to each other, how we should handle money, how we can deal with difficult people and so forth. All of this is important for marriages as well as other relationships, and for that reason Proverbs is a great resource for navigating life in general and married life in particular.

But if you should ask the father of the book of Proverbs what is the single most important thing he has taught his son about marriage, the response would be surprising. He tells his son that the key to a healthy, strong marriage is that the son needs to love another woman even more than his wife.

Again, remember that we as readers of the book of Proverbs need to place ourselves in the place of the son. So whether we are married or single, male or female, we need to imagine we are the son. Husbands and wives must love this woman even more than their spouse. Single people must love her more than any other person.

> *If you should ask the father of the book of Proverbs what is the single most important thing he has taught his son about marriage, the response would be surprising.*

Who is this woman? Her name is Wisdom, and she calls out to people from her place on the highest point of the city. Let's read Proverbs 9:1-6:

Wisdom has built her house;
    she has carved its seven columns.
She has prepared a great banquet,
    mixed the wines, and set the table.
She has sent her servants to invite everyone to come.
    She calls out from the heights overlooking the city.
"Come in with me," she urges the simple.
    To those who lack good judgment, she says,
"Come, eat my food,
    and drink the wine I have mixed.
Leave your simple ways behind, and begin to live;
    learn to use good judgment."

In this passage young men are invited to Wisdom's house to eat. Now such an invitation in its ancient Near Eastern environment implies more than just enjoying good food. A man and woman eating a meal together suggests the development of a relationship on the most intimate terms. This fits in with the father's earlier advice to love and embrace Woman Wisdom in a place like 4:4-9.

Indeed, the first eight chapters come to a climax in chapter 9. All throughout this first part of the book, the father teaches his son using what might be called a two-path theology. There is the straight path that leads to life and a crooked path that leads to death. The father urges his son to stay on the straight path. Here in chapter 9 the path takes the young men past this high place from which Woman Wisdom invites him to dinner.

However, this is not the first time in Proverbs the reader has learned about Woman Wisdom. She first speaks in 1:20-33, and the father is constantly commending this woman to his son. But the place we learn most about Woman Wisdom is chapter 8. Here, after an introduction (8:1-11), Wisdom herself speaks and tells us all about herself (8:12-26), and what we learn is impressive. I can give only a short and selective summary:

1. Wisdom is aligned with goodness and hates evil.
2. Wisdom was around before creation and witnessed how God constructed the world. This implies that she knows how to live in God's world.
3. She imparts wisdom and insight to those who listen to her, and they will experience joy and life, while those who reject her will suffer and die.
    But all that said, who is this woman?

Before we answer this we have to take notice of her rival. Woman Wisdom is not the only one issuing dinner invitations in chapter 9. Listen to the rival invitation from Woman Folly:

> The woman named Folly is brash.
>> She is ignorant and doesn't know it.
> She sits in her doorway
>> on the heights overlooking the city.
> She calls out to men going by
>> who are minding their own business.
> "Come in with me," she urges the simple.
>> To those who lack good judgment, she says,
> "Stolen water is refreshing;
>> food eaten in secret tastes the best!"
> But little do they know that the dead are there.
>> Her guests are in the depths of the grave. (9:13-18)

She too invites the men—us, the readers of Proverbs—to a meal. In other words, she too wants an intimate relationship with us. She too makes the promise of a delectable feast. It is tasty and refreshing.

Again, who are these women?

The passage is subtle but clear. The key to their identity is given in the location of their homes. They both live on "the heights overlooking the city."

But in ancient Israel and throughout the ancient Near East, whose house was on the heights? God's. Temples were built on the highest point. In Jerusalem, for instance, the temple was located on Mount Zion. In Mesopotamia, where there were no natural mountains, they built them in the form of stepped pyramids, called ziggurats, on the top of which were temples.

In other words, Woman Wisdom stands for Yahweh's Wisdom and ultimately God himself.

Then what about Woman Folly? She represents the false gods, the idols of the nations, who try to lure Israel away from the true God.

Thus you see that at the heart of Proverbs, at the end of the father's discourses to the son (chapters 1—9) and just before the lengthy series of pithy proverbs (chapters 10—31), we the reader, must make a fundamental choice. Will we enter into a relationship with Woman Wisdom (God) or Woman Folly (idols)? The decision has life-and-death consequences.

We husbands must love

another woman before

we can properly love

our wife, and you wives

must love her more and

before you can love

your husband.

As we think of Proverbs' teaching on the practical side of marriage, then, we must first acknowledge that we husbands must love another woman before we can properly love our wife, and you wives must love her more and before you can love your husband. As Proverbs puts the same truth in a more prosaic way elsewhere: "Fear of the LORD is the foundation of true knowledge" (1:7).

The first step in a strong marriage is to love God deeply and reject idols.

JESUS AND WOMAN WISDOM

Before we leave this fundamental point, we should read the decision of Proverbs 9 in the light of the New Testament. The surprising revelation of the New Testament is that Jesus fulfills the Old Testament. In regard to Proverbs, the New Testament makes it clear that we should associate *Jesus* with Woman Wisdom.

After all, it is Jesus who is the treasury of God's wisdom (Colossians 2:3). And because of this he is described in language reminiscent of the description of Proverbs 8 in texts like Colossians 1:15-20 and John 1. Then note a passage like Matthew 11:19, where he implies that his actions are the actions of Woman Wisdom.

My point is that for the Christian the choice in Proverbs 9 should be understood to be a choice between Jesus and anything else, any person or thing, that threatens to become an idol in our life.

Thus to have a strong marriage, we must build it on an even stronger relationship with Christ, and we need to encourage our spouse to do the same.

The Ideal Wife: An Echo of Woman Wisdom (Proverbs 31:10-31)

With this background, let's take a look at Proverbs' description of the ideal woman. She is the virtuous and capable wife of Proverbs 31:10-31 [read].

After I read this passage I often say to myself, *Wow, what a woman.* I sometimes suspect that the answer to the opening question, "Who can find a virtuous and capable wife?" is "No one," because there is no one who can measure up to this description!

It's not my purpose here to fully unpack this rich passage. I just want to make a few points and then commit it to you for your further reflection:

1. This form of poem is interesting and telling. It is what scholars call an acrostic. Every verse starts with a successive letter of the Hebrew alphabet. It is like an *A, B, C* description of the noble woman. Indeed, another way of looking at it is as an *A*-to-*Z* description.

2. This picture is an ideal composite. I do not think it is offered as a blueprint that every woman must follow. Some of the description involves requirements, but much of it is permission. Not every woman, for instance, needs to be involved in business as well as being active on the home front.

3. Even so, the picture in Proverbs 31 does debunk some of our stereotypes of the Israelite woman, and the Christian woman as well. This woman is an initiator, active in business and the community as well as effective in her home life. Not every woman needs to be wheeling and dealing in commerce, but this text allows for it. Responding to those who say that she is just engaged in commerce based in the home, I would point out that that was the way business worked at the time of Proverbs. They did not have multinational corporations with offices downtown.

Character of strong compassion, . . . courage as she reaches out to a torn world and most of all . . . deep trust in God are goals for all women and wives.

4. The noble woman cares for her family. She does not single-mindedly pursue her own happiness and career goals. Her efforts have as their goal the betterment of her family. Her husband benefits: "She brings him good, not harm" (31:12). She gets up early to prepare breakfast for her family. She is always thinking of the future, so when trouble comes she is ready. Her work allows her husband to thrive at work as well. He praises her in the city gate. At the conclusion of the poem, her children also praise her.

5. Most important, the virtuous and capable woman loves God. Verse 30 puts it bluntly: "Charm is deceptive, and beauty does not last; / but a woman who fears the LORD will be greatly praised."

These words are among the last of the whole poem and really provide the foundation for the rest. The hymn places charm and beauty in their proper perspective. Human beauty is not evil, and charm does not have to be deceptive. But when they are, they should be scorned. Beauty and sincere charm should be admired, but only for what they are. Without faith, beauty and charm are totally worthless. They are repulsive.

Proverbs 31:10-31 is thus a hymn of a noble woman, a godly woman. While the picture is vivid because it presents a woman from a particular culture and social class, her character of strong compassion, her courage as she reaches out to a torn world and most of all her deep trust in God are goals for all women and wives.

The Ideal Husband: Psalm 112

Now as I said, Proverbs is addressed to young men, and sometimes I can imagine women feel a bit picked on in the book. But there is a counterpart to Proverbs 31 outside the book of Proverbs that is often missed. It describes the man who fears the Lord, and it too is an acrostic, an *A*-to-*Z* of the godly man.

[Read Psalm 112. Note: if a gender-inclusive translation is used—for example, NRSV, TNIV, NLT, NCV—then the minister will have to point out that it is a *man* that is meant here.]

Like Proverbs 31, Psalm 112 puts pride of place to the fear of the Lord (verse 1). The godly man will not fear other people because his fear is in the Lord. In the light of the fear of God, all other fears fade into insignificance. The godly man fears no one and nothing except God.

The psalm links the fear of the Lord with obedience to his commands. The opening of Psalm 112 is similar to the beginning of Psalm 1; both begin with "Blessed is the man" and then describe a person who obeys God's law.

Even though we New Testament Christians read these verses through the eyes of grace, the law still plays an important role in our lives. It expresses God's will for us. In plain language, the law, as expressed in the Ten Commandments, tells us how to live in a way that pleases God. The law is our guideline for how to live a life of gratitude.

Psalm 112 describes such a grateful man. He is in relationship with God and expresses his thanks by joyful observance of God's law. A godly man is a Word-centered man. He loves the Word of God and draws his ethics, passion and hope from what is revealed in Scripture.

Like the godly woman, the godly man has an unshakable confidence in the future. This is the case though the psalm also recognizes that life is a battle. The man is a warrior who goes out into daily life ready to encounter the forces of darkness that seek to undo him and those around him. However, he is secure because he knows that God will bring him the victory in the end.

Few men have this type of confidence today. We feel that our world is more dangerous, complex and difficult than the world of Israelite men. In some ways perhaps this is true, but not in others. Ancient Israelite men faced many forces that threatened their existence and the safety of their family. Famine could hit without warning. War was a near-constant phenomenon in the ancient world. Disease could ravage the countryside, and corrupt, unchecked government officials could destroy a man's life. Nonetheless, the godly man of Psalm 112 has no fear of bad news because his fear is in the Lord. Notice that the psalm assumes that life will bring him bad news. It will bring him trouble. But his confidence in the Lord keeps him going.

Because he lacks fear and has confidence in the future, he is no miser with his own wealth (verse 9). Like the godly woman, the godly man is generous toward the poor.

A godly man is a Word-centered man. He loves the Word of God and draws his ethics, passion and hope from what is revealed in Scripture.

———— r ————

Again and again, Proverbs bombards us with the following counsel: to cultivate a strong marriage, a wife and husband must individually and together cultivate a deep and abiding relationship with God. To fear the Lord shows that you understand your proper place in the universe. You are a creature, dependent for everything on your Creator.

Why is it so important to found our marriage relationship on a relationship with Christ? Because our spouse will always let us down. If we make our husband or wife the most important person in our life rather than God, we create an idol that will never be able to come through for us. Proverbs 31 and Psalm 112 are ideals toward which we are prayerfully to strive, but this side of heaven no mortal can achieve them.

We remain sinners even after our conversion, and often our sin is harm directed toward our spouse. Our more fundamental relationship with Woman Wisdom, that is, God himself, who never lets us down, gives us the power not just to weather the storm of an intimate relationship between two sinners but to grow together as we repent and forgive each other. We point each other toward the ultimate goal, which is to be like Christ, who is as we have seen Wisdom himself.

Let's end with the father's appeal to his son to make Woman Wisdom the love of his life (Proverbs 4:1-9):

> My children, listen when your father corrects you.
>> Pay attention and learn good judgment,
> for I am giving you good guidance.
>> Don't turn away from my instructions.
> For I, too, was once my father's son,
>> tenderly loved as my mother's only child.
>
> My father taught me,
>> "Take my word to heart.
>> Follow my commands, and you will live.
> Get wisdom; develop good judgment.
>> Don't forget my words or turn away from them.
> Don't turn your back on wisdom, for she will protect you.
>> Love her, and she will guard you.
> Getting wisdom is the wisest thing you can do!
>> And whatever else you do, develop good judgment.
> If you prize wisdom, she will make you great.
>> Embrace her, and she will honor you.
> She will place a lovely wreath on your head;
>> she will present you with a beautiful crown.

SERMON THREE: LOVE RESTORED
SONG OF SONGS 4:1—5:1

Our Scripture reading this morning is from the Song of Songs. Now I need to warn those of you who have not yet spent time in this book that this passage is pretty hot stuff. Indeed, the book is so sensuous that many pastors are hesitant to preach from the Song.

But to neglect the Song of Songs from the pulpit is a mistake, and it may be one explanation for why Christians are so confused about sexuality. First of all, let me point out the obvious. God put it in the canon. That means it is for the church. We need to preach from the whole of God's Word, including those portions that may make us feel uncomfortable. Second, the Song presents a positive, God-honoring perspective on marital sex-

uality. If the church wants to combat the sexual idolatry of our culture, it cannot do so by simply
repressing and discouraging sex. It can combat sexual idolatry only by presenting the Bible's view of a
vibrant marital sexuality. The Song of Songs is God's
resource for doing this.

Getting wisdom is the wisest thing you can do! And whatever else you do, develop good judgment. If you prize wisdom, she will make you great.

🄡

We have already seen in our study of Genesis 2:24
that God envisions marriage as having three parts:
leaving, weaving and cleaving. Song of Songs celebrates marital cleaving.

As we will see, the Song of Songs is for the whole
church, not just married people, but it is true that
only married people can act on the sensuous feelings
that the book evokes. Even so, singles can benefit
from hearing about marriage from the Song. As a
matter of fact, singles are represented in the Song by
a group of women who occasionally speak; they are
called the Daughters of Jerusalem.

There are only three voices in the Song, those of an
unnamed man and an unnamed woman and the
Daughters of Jerusalem. They serve more than one
role in the book, but an important one is that they are the woman's disciples in love. She
uses her actions and speech to teach them about the joys and dangers of sexuality. More
than once in the book the woman will turn to them and say, as in 3:5,

> Promise me, O women of Jerusalem,
>> by the gazelles and wild deer,
>> not to awaken love until the time is right.

So singles, listen and learn, but also wait for God's timing.

Now speaking to you married couples, I know you are not all alike. Some of you are
pretty happy with your relationship, including your sexual relationship. The Song may
be a catalyst for enriching your pleasure. For some of you, the fire of your marriage has
gone out. Listen to the Song and use it to rekindle that passion.

The point is whether you are single, divorced, widowed, or married for one day or
fifty years, sexuality is a huge part of your life. We feel all kinds of pressures and tensions
and confusion. Society says, "Get rid of your inhibitions." The church often has a subtle

The point is whether you

are single, divorced,

widowed, or married for

one day or fifty years,

sexuality is a huge part

of your life.

🜸

message that we ought to repress our sexuality and sometimes an explicit message that sex and the body get in the way of our spirituality. The Song of Songs will prove to be a corrective to both viewpoints.

Understanding the Song of Songs

[Read Song of Songs 4:1—5:1.]

To understand any part of the Song of Songs, one needs an orientation to the whole book. For centuries the Song was taken as an allegory—that is, a poem not about human love but about the love of God for his people. Jewish readers took the book as an expression of God's love (represented by the man) toward Israel (the woman). They then read the details of the poem and conformed them to this overarching approach. Thus Song of Songs 1:2-4 says:

> Kiss me and kiss me again,
>   for your love is sweeter than wine.
> How fragrant your cologne;
>   your name is like its spreading fragrance.
>   No wonder all the young women love you!
> Take me with you; come, let's run!
>   The king has brought me into his bedroom.

Here we have the woman (Israel) asking the man (God) to take her into his bedroom (the Promised Land). Thus almost magically this love poem turns into a description of the exodus.

Christian interpreters believed that the man was Jesus and the woman was the church or the individual Christian. Then they pressed the details. For instance, Song of Songs 1:13: "My lover is like a sachet of myrrh / lying between my breasts." This was taken by Christian interpreters since Cyril of Alexandria (c. A.D. 200) as referring to Christ (the sachet) who spans the Old and New Testaments (the two breasts).

Most readers today would recognize these interpretations as quite fanciful. What led interpreters to such lengths? Well, they were shocked by the sexual content of the Song. Living under the influence of a foreign philosophy (Platonism) that argued that the physical (body) and the spiritual (soul) are two separate things, they had to adopt an interpretive method (allegory) that made the text say something other than what it obviously said on the surface.

Today, one would find it difficult to name a biblical scholar or theologian who would take such a view. Virtually everyone recognizes that the Song is a poem that celebrates (and occasionally warns about) the physical love between a woman and a man.

However, among these interpreters there is another debate. Does the Song tell a story? Interpretations that take the Song as telling the story of a particular couple as they meet, date, get married, have a honeymoon and so forth are popular today. Yet there are as many different stories discovered in the Song as there are interpreters. That is because it is easy to create a story in a poem like the Song.

It is much better to simply affirm the Song for what it is: a poem, or better yet a collection of poems. They are lyric poems that celebrate love, and our job is to unpack the many images that it uses and apply them to our marriages.

And that is what we will do today with Song of Songs 4:1—5:1.

A Descriptive Love Poem

This text is a particular type of love poem. You may be interested to know that the form has survived down to modern times in Arabic poetry. It is called a *wasf*, or descriptive poem, and it is sung at weddings as a prelude to lovemaking—remember, I said this was pretty hot stuff. In this type of *wasf*, the man describes the beauty of his wife, from head to—well, you'll just have to wait to see. Elsewhere in the Song, there is a similar poem where the woman describes how attractive her husband is from the head down.

As we unpack the images of the chapter, they often strike us as strange, even funny. As we will see, these aren't compliments that we can transfer directly to our relationships, but they do tell us that it is biblical to encourage our spouse by telling them just how attractive we find them. The Song is the biblical invitation, perhaps even mandate, for complimenting our spouse.

It is also a mandate for *receiving* compliments. The Song gives a corrective to a false kind of humility. Some of us find it hard to hear compliments about our attractiveness. We may even respond to them by

> *The Song is the biblical invitation, perhaps even mandate, for complimenting our spouse.*

quoting Proverbs 31:30: "Charm is deceptive, and beauty does not last; / but a woman who fears the LORD will be greatly praised."

But note that this verse does not say that beauty is totally unimportant. It puts it in its proper place. The most important thing is fear of the Lord, but how wonderful it is that my wife both loves God and is beautiful in my eyes.

Unpacking the Metaphors

As I now highlight some of the powerful metaphors that this passage presents to us, let me point out just how sensuous they are. Every sense is appealed to. The beloved is beautiful to the man's sight, her scent drives him wild, he wants to touch her, her voice is appealing.

He begins with her head. One's face is unique, and hers is partly hidden by a veil. There is nothing more intriguing than a partially hidden beauty. It enhances one's desire.

The metaphorical description of her teeth is illustrative of the fact that we can't just transfer these compliments to our spouse today. Noting the fact that she has all her teeth may have been quite a compliment in the Old Testament period, but it doesn't work to-day with our improved dental hygiene.

Her lips are described in a way that makes it quite clear what he wants to do. He wants to kiss her deeply.

The image of her neck as the tower of David ringed by shields must be understood in relation to the practice of hanging ornamental shields on the outside of a fortified tower. This would be similar to a beautiful necklace around a dignified neck. It also is a good example of the frequent use in the Song of military images to celebrate the woman's beauty. Her beauty is the type that mesmerizes and makes one's knees knock.

The image of the breasts like two fawns grazing among the lilies is frequently misconceived. One must picture the scene not head first but rear first. We are looking at the rounded rears of the fawns with their nipplelike tails proudly protruding into the air as the fawns lean forward to graze. There is nothing prudish about this biblical love poem, and it encourages Christian married couples into the same loving openness. It invites sensuous love talk.

But skipping down to the end of the chapter, there is nothing more sensuous than the man's ecstatic description of the woman's garden fountain. This is the ultimate object of his loving attention and shows us that this poem is the man's verbal foreplay to intimate lovemaking. In the ancient Near East the garden, and in particular the garden well or fountain, is metaphorical of the most private part of a woman's body. He desires to enter this garden, but he also praises her for being a *private* garden, a *secluded* spring, a *hidden* fountain.

At this point the man's speech ends and the woman responds (4:16). To his great joy, she invites him to enter her garden and "taste" its finest fruits! She opens up to her husband.

And according to 5:1 he wastes no time in responding. He enthusiastically and fully enjoys her garden ("I drink wine with my milk").

Finally, the chorus chimes in affirming their love in the second half of 5:1. Everyone is happy:

Oh, lover and beloved, eat and drink!
Yes, drink deeply of your love!

Thus the Song celebrates the physical love of a man and his wife. It invites and encourages Christian couples to play together, to enjoy each other's body. Marital sexual intimacy is God's gift.

Sex as Idol and Taboo

There is a reason that God in his wisdom included these love poems in the canon. God is concerned about you. He is concerned about the whole you, and that includes your body. Sometimes we fall into the trap of separating our soul, which we tend to think of in terms of an invisible thing dwelling inside our body, from our body, and we believe that God is concerned only about our soul. Nothing could be further from the truth of the Bible. God created our bodies. He takes care of our bodies now, and he will resurrect our bodies.

> **God is concerned about you. He is concerned about the whole you, and that includes your body.**

Our sexuality is an important part of our bodily life. As a matter of fact, it is an integral part of our life. We tend to compartmentalize our sex life. We believe it is a slice of the pie. Actually it permeates our whole life. This explains some of the emotions we feel in marriage. If you have a sexual problem, it affects your whole marriage, and if there is a nonsexual problem between you, it affects your sexual relationship. Let's say that, reversing the stereotype, the husband is cold sexually toward his wife. This leads to frustration on her part and anger in the relationship. Or on the other hand, let's say the husband forgot to fix something in the house for the twelfth week in a row. Resentment builds up so that a healthy sexual relationship is not possible between the husband and the wife.

We could illustrate this in a number of ways, and in your life it may be different from any example I might give, but becoming aware of the fact that our sexual life, our body life and our spiritual life are all integrated and not different sections of our life will help us to grapple with our problems. A sexual problem is not usually just sexual but often serves as an indication of a relationship problem.

But it may be that a sexual problem has led to the broader problem. We live in a sinful world. Sexuality was created good and beautiful, but our sin has warped our perceptions and experience of it. We tend to make sex either an idol or a taboo—either of which will lead to major problems.

We must never forget that God created us male and female and made us to be companions of one other.

On the one hand, we are tempted to make sex an idol. There is no doubt about it; we are living in a morally loose age. We are being bombarded by sexual literature, movies and so on all the time. Sex is a major obsession of our society. Our society promotes the idea that life without some type of sexual stimulation is boring at least, meaningless at most. What has happened is that sex has been made an idol. An idol is anything that God created which human beings take and promote to the level of the Creator (Romans 1:21-22). The simple fact is that human beings have rejected the Creator and have replaced God with sex. You can see why sex makes such an attractive idol. People believe that it can fill up the loneliness that a lack of meaningful relationship with God creates.

Even Christians who are married may make an idol out of sex within marriage. First Corinthians 7:4-5 says, "The wife gives authority over her body to her husband, and the husband gives authority over his body to his wife. Do not deprive each other of sexual relations," and sometimes Christians use this text like a sledgehammer. We must be sensitive to our spouse in this area and not force them into a schedule of sexual encounters that would soon take all the joy out of that relationship.

Yes, sex can be and is made an idol, but it can also be perverted when it is made taboo. You can make it an idol by putting it in the place of the Creator. You can make it a taboo by forgetting that God created our bodies with our sexual organs and we were made to enjoy this good gift of God's creation. We must never forget that God created us male and female and made us to be companions of one other. The Song is a biblical reminder that sex is good and pleasurable. It is not evil when enjoyed within the confines of marriage. Christians past and present have often treated sex as some type of necessary evil. Once again, this is a result of a misconception regarding God's love for us. He loves us body and spirit.

Sex is not a duty, created only for the purpose of continuing the race or, from a Christian perspective, as one of my friends in seminary used to say, "to make the church grow larger." It is something to enjoy. And certainly the woman and the man in the Song are enjoying one another's body.

There are taboos in sex. Scripture is explicit about sexual sin, bestiality, adultery, prostitution and so forth. But don't throw out the blessings of God's gift of sexuality because of the perversion of sin. That's exactly what Satan would rejoice in. Learn from the Song—sex is good, enjoy it within marriage.

If you and your spouse are having difficulties in your sexual relationship, don't just sweep it under the rug, believing that the rest of your relationship will stand firm. Talk with one another, and seek help from counselors of the church. Otherwise this problem that you've compartmentalized will eat away at the very foundation of your marriage.

The Redemption of Sexuality

Think about the message of this poem in the context of the Scriptures as a whole. It is purposefully reminding you of the story of the Garden of Eden in Genesis 2. There, Adam and Eve are naked and feeling no shame (2:25). But in the very next chapter, after their willful disobedience in eating the fruit of the tree, they must cover themselves up. They are no longer comfortably naked—physically, emotionally, spiritually—before the other. Reading in the light of these passages, we see in the Song that the man and the woman are in the garden again, naked and enjoying themselves. The message of the Song, then, has to do with the redemption of broken sexuality.

If time permitted I would develop another aspect of the teaching of the Song, but I need to just mention it here. The redemption of sexuality is an already-but-not-yet redemption, and the Song includes other poems (such as the one that follows in 5:2—6:3) indicating that not even a husband and wife always easily and fully move toward each other with intimacy.

Still, the major teaching of the Song is the possibility of wonderful, exciting sexual enjoyment. It is an invitation for married couples to kindle a passionate relationship. God wants you to enjoy each other.

I have heard Christians say that the Bible teaches that love is not an emotion but rather a commitment. Now I know what they are saying, and their purpose is good. One does not stay in or leave a marriage based on the level of emotional passion one feels. No marriage is simply a commitment made by two people in love; if the feeling fades, that is no reason to end a marriage. However, it is quite wrong to think that the Bible is not interested in romance. If God is unhappy with a divorce, he is also unhappy with a passionless marriage.

It is quite wrong to think that the Bible is not interested in romance. If God is unhappy with a divorce, he is also unhappy with a passionless marriage.

It is common to hear that the institution of marriage is under unprecedented attack today, and indeed that is true. But you know, marriage has always been in danger, even when there were few divorces. When there were few divorces there were many loveless marriages.

What could we really expect? Marriage brings together two sinners. That is a formula for conflict. But the Song's message is that strong and exciting marriages are possible. Other Scriptures teach us that they are possible when the gospel is applied to marriages. That is where sin is owned (repentance), forgiveness is offered and reconciliation takes place.

In other words, truly strong marriage relationships must be built on the gospel. How can we deal with the sin of a spouse unless we also recognize our own sin (the log in our own eye) and that both of us have been forgiven by Christ? The gospel is the story of an abundant and overwhelming forgiveness in light of sin. Jesus Christ made the ultimate sacrifice and died for our sins on the cross. His forgiveness saves us from our guilt and sin as well as giving us the promise of eternal life with him forever. What people don't understand is that this pattern of exposure, repentance and forgiveness, far from dampening love, fuels it.

The message of the Song of Songs is a message of hope for marriages and an invitation to express that hope through the passionate love engendered between a husband and a wife.

SERMON FOUR: A SURVIVAL GUIDE TO MARRIAGE—THE PLANK AND THE SPECK
MATTHEW 7:1-5

Marriage is the most intense of all human relationships. It is the crucible for the greatest joy and the most devastating heartache. It is exciting, yet it can be tedious. It can be a source of support in the midst of a chaotic, dangerous and dark world, or it can contribute to the turmoil of a fallen world. Usually it does both to some degree.

Anyone who says their marriage is perfect is either lying or incredibly superficial. I remember good advice from the Christian counselor Jay Adams. It was from a talk he gave to engaged couples, and I heard it years ago right after getting engaged myself. He asked the young couples in the audience what they expected from marriage. He knew they thought that marriage would be the answer to some of their most pressing desires and anxieties. Once they were married, loneliness would not be a problem. Sexual frustration would be a thing of the past. Bliss and joy awaited them. Adams did not pull any punches. He made his point by reminding us that marriage united two sinners and that such a union does not solve the sin problem but accentuates it.

I speak as someone who naturally prefers the apparent problem-free life of the superficial. Fortunately I was engaged to a woman who refuses to remain superficial. In the first few months of our dating relationship, we didn't have a single fight. It seemed as if she could do no wrong and I could do no wrong. But one day, out of nowhere, she picked a fight. She purposefully found a topic that could lead us into conflict, and she kept at it till I exploded.

Later she told me that she had done this in order to see whether I was capable of more than a superficial relationship and to see how I would handle conflict. A very wise woman, but not always easy to live with.

The Pervasiveness of Sin

If the Bible is true, then there is no perfect marriage. If the Bible is true, then every husband and wife will have stories to tell about conflicts, minor and major, in their relationship. After all, as we learn from Genesis 3, everyone is a sinner, all of us are people who look out for ourselves. Listen to Romans 3:23: "Everyone has sinned; we all fall short of God's glorious standard." No one is an exception. No one can say, "I am not a sinner" (see also Romans 5:9-20).

At its heart sin is a refusal to trust God.

But what is sin? At its heart sin is a refusal to trust

God. Sin is when we rely on anything but God for our lives. In other words, we sin when we go against God's will as it is stated in the Bible. Sin also looks out for the self, and since marriage requires a mutual submission (Ephesians 5:21), a mutual considering the other as more important than oneself, sin is a tremendous problem, alienating two people who are supposed to be one flesh.

And marriage has some areas where conflict routinely arises. While I don't have time to go into any of these in great detail, just naming them will bring such conflicts to mind.

Triggers of Conflict Within Marriage

Sex. We are sexual beings. God created us with a desire for intimate physical touch. The desire is powerful, but a pair of spouses may not share the same level of desire all the time. Sometimes the man will move toward the woman and she moves away. Sometimes she will move toward him and he moves away. The Song of Songs has a poem describing a situation where sexual connection is difficult (5:2—6:3).

Limited time and money. We are finite creatures with finite resources. Time and money are two resources that most often expose our limits and failures. Conflicts over time and money are really over personal values. They are conflicts over what time and money *mean.* We give our money and time to those things that are most important to us and that reveal our deepest values. Money and time represent power—the ability to do things and to influence people. Do we budget for education or for vacations? Do we buy clothes or season tickets to the football team?

Time becomes a commodity of contention as well. Should a wife work, which might require her husband to take care of the kids after he gets home from his job? Is the husband spending too much time at work rather than with his wife and children? A fight over who is going to pick up the kids is a fight over whose time is more valuable.

Divided loyalties. Our primary loyalty, of course, is toward God. Look at the disaster that Solomon perpetrated when he chose a marriage that betrayed that fundamental loyalty [read 1 Kings 11:1-6].

Paul talks about this in principle in a way that speaks to all intimate relationships, certainly including marriage [read 2 Corinthians 6:14-16].

However, after our relationship with God, our primary relationship is to our spouse. Troubles arise if other relationships begin to take the place our marriage should hold. We can talk about parents, and of course friends sometimes supersede a spouse in importance, but probably the relationships that most often replace marriage as primary are those with our children.

After all, children need our support, time and attention. Our spouse is an adult and can understand why our attention has to be directed primarily toward the children. I think this kind of thinking is wrong and detrimental not only to the relationship but to the children, because their parents' bad or troubled marriage will affect the children negatively. Children need their parents to have a strong, healthy relationship.

Commitment and Romance

It is when the marriage relationship is threatened by tensions and sin that we need to remember that the relationship is more than romance. Notice I did not say that marriage *has nothing to do with* romance and feeling. There is an erroneous idea out there that romantic love is foreign to the Bible. People who say that must never have read the Song of Songs! The Bible understands our marriage relationships to be the matrix of intense, passionate feelings of love.

To be realistic, the flame does not burn white-hot all the time, and sometimes it is quite cold. But still the relationship stands.

Marriage, after all, is covenant [read Malachi 2:13-16].

A covenant is a legal agreement to stick by each other in thick or thin. This is why divorce should never be easy for a Christian, even in those situations allowed by Scripture.

But fine, how does this not simply lead to a committed, passionless relationship—or even worse, a relationship in which the spouses dislike or even hate each other because of past offenses and annoyances?

The biblical pattern for a healthy and robust marriage is acknowledgment of failure and forgiveness freely given.

Repentance and Forgiveness

The answer is repentance and forgiveness. The biblical pattern for a healthy and robust marriage is acknowledgment of failure and forgiveness freely given.

The gospel gives us a pattern for living in relationship in a sinful world. We must know our sin as we also forgive the sins of others. [Read Matthew 7:1-5.]

This passage does not absolutely forbid judging other people. If it did that, it would contradict a number of other passages that not only give permission but actually encourage Christians to help each other discover and deal with sin in their lives (Luke 17:3; Galatians 6:1; 1 Timothy 5:20). What it does prohibit is a proud judgment, a judgment that does not allow me to recognize the sin in my own life. A proud judgment allows me to use my wife's sin to crush her rather than build her up.

We sin daily against each other. But this is not bad news. Jack Miller, a prolific author who was once my pastor, used to say all the time, "Cheer up, you are a lot worse than you think!" What he meant was that our sin was extensive and he was calling us to recognize this and to repent daily. It's good news because God's grace is continually present to us. If it weren't for the forgiveness of God through Christ, our failures would utterly destroy us. But our hope and confidence are based not on our goodness but on divine forgiveness.

It is right and good for Alice and me to deal gently and compassionately with each other's faults. Together we can help each other grow into maturity in the faith.

Some of you may remember the 1970s movie *Love Story*, which popularized the saying "Love means never having to say you're sorry." This is worse than trite; it can destroy a relationship. The opposite is true: love means *constantly* saying you are sorry.

But we must be mindful: Jesus teaches that I must know that my sin is greater than my wife's sin. She has a speck; I have a plank. She must have the same perspective from her side. If we both approach each other's speck knowing that we have logs, then we can approach each other with the attitude that will win each other to Christ.

Unremitting Forgiveness

And our forgiveness is to be unremitting. [Read Luke 17:3-4.]

These verses show that though we must first recognize our own sins, a wife and husband should still tenderly expose each other's faults. Our approach must be tender: such exposure can be painful, since sin is ugly and none of us like to be exposed. Think how embarrassed we feel when someone tells us that we have a piece of lettuce dangling from our lip. How much more shameful is the exposure of sin.

We need to expose sin tenderly because such exposure is not intended to ridicule or hurt the other but to restore and strengthen our relationship. Jesus here teaches that our forgiveness should be unending toward those who come to us broken and sorry for their offenses.

Marriage does bring two people together into a lifelong intimate relationship, where repetitive offense can happen. There will be times when a wife or husband is tempted to say, "Enough is enough!"

But by using the number seven, which stands for completion, Jesus tells his disciples that our forgiveness never ends. There is never a point where we can say "That's the 1,034th time you've hurt me this way. That's it. I'm leaving."

People wrongly think that many faults can only destroy a marriage. And they can, unless we adopt a forgiving attitude stemming from the recognition that my faults are greater than my spouse's.

Forgiveness Enhances Love

According to the gospel, though, the reverse is true: forgiveness enhances love. If my wife can live with me in spite of my faults, then she must really love me. When I offend her, she still stays with me! Now that is deep and abiding love.

[Read Luke 7:46-47.] In reference to Simon's charge that the woman who just poured oil on Jesus' feet was a great sinner, Jesus responds that she loves much because she has been forgiven much. Being the recipient of forgiveness fuels love.

Such a relationship also breaks through pretense—our flimsy attempts to hide from each other our problems and faults. If we know that our spouse is a forgiving person, then we are more apt to be open about our struggles.

What hope then is there for marriage in a fallen world? Jesus Christ is the hope that brings joy in the present and certainty about the future.

What hope then is there for marriage in a fallen world? Jesus Christ is the hope that brings joy in the present and certainty about the future. Jesus is the One who gives us the grace that allows us to acknowledge our own sins and also to forgive the sins of our spouse. The lifestyle of repentance and forgiveness gives us hope for joy in the present.

It does not come easily, because we are all self-defensive, especially early in marriage, but we need to cultivate relationships in which exposure of sins and faults can happen because we are ready with forgiveness tempered with the realization that we have our own faults.

MARRIAGE DRAMA

Zucchini Surprise

WRITTEN BY PETER MAYER

Note: Here is a drama that you can use to introduce the themes of leaving, cleaving and weaving in worship or to a group. It particularly emphasizes the theme of leaving your family of origin.

Setting: The Loman's home—late afternoon

A couple, the Lomans, in their thirties, arrive home through the front door. Suitcases in hand, they look like they have just gotten back from a short vacation.

JIM: *(to no one in particular)* We're home!

TRUDY: Madison, Madison! Come here girl!

JIM: That's funny. She usually is waiting by the door ready to pounce. I swear that cat is just like a dog.

TRUDY: Your mother probably scared her into early hibernation.

Jim gives Trudy a look.

TRUDY: I'm sorry. *(As if repeating a mantra)* It was nice of her to housesit and take care of Madison while we were gone.

JIM: It sure was. If she didn't bail us out, I don't what we would have done with your cat.

TRUDY: She's your cat too.

Trudy hangs up her coat in the hall closet.

TRUDY: Are you hungry? I've got a hankering for a grilled cheese sandwich and some tomato soup. How does that sound?

JIM: Sounds good to me.

Jim picks up the mail and starts flipping through it as Trudy exits to the kitchen.

Setting: Kitchen

Trudy walks in and immediately sees a large bowl filled with eleven freshly picked zucchinis. There is a large note in front of the bowl that says, "Fresh from my garden."

TRUDY: Of course. Why am I not surprised?

Trudy continues moving over to the cupboards. She opens one as if to pull something out but then stops and stares inside. Confused, she opens another cupboard, then another and then another. She slams the last one.

TRUDY: (screaming) Aaaahhhhhhhhhhh!

Jim is in the other room.

JIM: What!?

TRUDY: I can't believe it!

Jim enters the kitchen.

JIM: What?

TRUDY: She has gone too far this time!

JIM: What?

TRUDY: Your mother!

JIM: What did she do this time?

TRUDY: She completely rearranged my kitchen.

JIM: It looks the same to me.

TRUDY: She switched everything around. My pots are over here, and my dishes are over here.

Trudy walks over to the other side of the kitchen.

TRUDY: My Tupperware is all the way over here.

JIM: How do you know she did it?

TRUDY: Oh well, I guess it could have been a burglar who broke in just to rearrange
           my Tupperware. Or perhaps our furry cat Madison . . .

JIM: OK, point taken.

TRUDY: Well that's it! The kid gloves are off!

Trudy walks over to the phone picks it up. Jim tries to stop her.

JIM: Wait, don't do anything rash.

TRUDY: Why not? She invades our lives constantly, and you never do a thing about it.

JIM: That's not true.

TRUDY: Did you do anything when she bought us that ugly pink couch for our living
           room even when we told her not to? Or when we invited her over for dinner
           and she insisted on showing me how to cook the chicken?

Trudy walks over and grabs a zucchini and starts shaking it.

TRUDY: Or any of the times she unloads her mass quantities of zucchinis on us even
           though we tell her we don't like zucchini?

JIM: What am I supposed to do? She's my mother.

TRUDY: I need you to stick up for me—for us. Stand up to her. Tell her to back off.

JIM: That will only make things worse. You know how she is.

TRUDY: I do, and that's why I need you to do something.

JIM: What am I supposed to do?

TRUDY: I need to know that I come first before her.

JIM: What do you expect me to do: choose between you and my mother?

TRUDY: I just need to know that I—that we—come first.

Jim pauses, in deep thought.

JIM: You do. We come first.

TRUDY: Really? You mean that?

Jim walks to her and holds her.

JIM: Yes, I do.

TRUDY: Will you talk to her about the kitchen being off limits?

JIM: I'll talk to her at the first opportunity I can get. Deal?

TRUDY: Deal.

They hug for a long moment. They finally separate.

TRUDY: Well, I better get dinner going.

JIM: I'll take the suitcases upstairs.

As Trudy starts pulling a frying pan out, the phone rings.

Jim goes to pick it up.

JIM: Hello. *(Pause)* Oh, hi Mom! Yes, we had a great trip. *(Pauses as if listening)* Yes, everything at the house looks great. Thanks for taking care of things.

Trudy pauses for a moment in shock.

TRUDY: Ahhhhhh!

Trudy tosses the frying pan back into the cupboard, gives Jim a knowing glare then exits the kitchen fuming. Jim sort of reels from the shock.

JIM: *(talking into the phone)* Oh nothing, nothing.

He pauses for a moment, realizing what happened.

JIM: *(again into the phone)* Actually Mom, we need to talk. It's about the kitchen . . .